MINI MEALS IN MINUTES

by JUNE ROTH

Consultant: Rochelle Narotsky, Home Economist, *Hamilton Beach*

Dorison House Publishers, Inc., New York

Copyright © 1977 by Dorison House Publishers, Inc.

*Published by Dorison House Publishers, Inc.
183 Madison Avenue, New York, N.Y. 10016*

ISBN: 0-916752-09-7

Library of Congress Catalog Card Number 76-53111

Manufactured in the United States of America

Acknowledgment
Sincere thanks to Charlotte Adams, who contributed
considerably to the formulation of this book.

Interior illustrations by John Romer

Contents

Introduction

Fast cookers are new little electric appliances that can neatly grill or fry small amounts of food in a matter of minutes. They're the perfect answer to the problems of cooking for one or two people who are living life too fully to spend hours in the kitchen, but who prefer start-from-scratch meals at home to fast food on the run. Once you try a fast cooker you'll wonder why someone didn't have the good sense to invent them before! They are called "Little Mac", "Double Mac" and "Fry All".

The beauty of these fast cookers is that they can cook small quantities quickly and save you time when cleaning up. The "Double Mac" lives up to its name, providing ample space to cook two sandwiches, two hamburgers, or even tempura for two. Its relative, the "Little Mac", does the same for one. Whichever you use, you can cook easier and better from now on than you ever did before.

The clever design permits the top lid of each appliance to become an open grill. Lock it in place and it serves as a hot lid that clamps down on a square plate for sandwiches or a round plate for hamburgers. Just a minute or two on each side and the cooking's all done. Sort of like a fascinating kitchen toy—but much more fun! You'll find that fast cookers save energy because you can make a meal in minutes. Good for those who are serious about conserving electricity, because you couldn't cook faster any other way.

Food tastes better, too, when it's cooked right on the spot just before meal time. The nutrients are sealed right in, along with tasty juices and vitamins, when you use one of these little fast cookers. All are thermostatically controlled to reach just the right heat to do the job with precision—no chance of precious nutrients seeping out, with these searing techniques.

The grill lids of the "Mac" fast cookers need only a gentle wiping and they're clean and ready for the next use. The lower cooking plates swish clean with a dunking in detergent, then just rinse and wipe. They're both lightweight and portable.

Great time and money savers when you're away from home, whether studying, traveling, or on vacation. They travel back and forth easily, giving you a meal in minutes wherever there's a handy plug. How satisfying to have a hot food supply at your fingertips to meet your needs of hunger and good health!

The "Fry All" is a tiny deep fat fryer which holds two and one-half cups of oil that can be cooled and stored right in the appliance, ready for reuse whenever you're in the mood for crisply fried fish, chicken, fritters or dough-nuts. You'll find hundreds of ways to put this handy little utensil to work—like making hors d'oeuvres to be dunked into tasty dips or making your own potato chips. Whatever you choose, the oil gets hot enough to brown the outside of the food without penetrating the interior—the secret of perfect frying every time.

SOME THINGS YOU SHOULD KNOW

All recipes in this book specify whether cooking is to be done on the cover grill, in the closed unit or in the deep fryer. Suggested cooking times are given to help you to anticipate when browning will occur.

It is a good idea to stay near the fast cooker to prevent overcooking while it is in use.

You can use the open grill without adding any fat to get a toasted sand-wich with dry toast. The addition of butter or oil makes a moister, tastier sandwich.

Where butter is specified margarine may be substituted. At times recipes call for half butter/half oil. The purpose of that, as French chefs well know, is to prevent the fat from burning, by way of the oil, and to give it good flavor, by the use of butter.

Avoid overcooking fish and chicken as they can get dry and tasteless. The object is to achieve moist and delicately browned food.

If the sandwich is too high to close the cover completely on a "Little Mac," place top cover and bottom tray at right angles to each other during cooking.

If cooking frozen food on the grill, add 1 or 2 minutes to the cooking time. If using frozen food in the covered unit, add 1 minute for each side.

For hamburgers, mix ½ cup ground beef with 2 teaspoons of filling such as catsup, green pepper, grated onion or relish. Place on preheated cooking plate and cook 1 minute for rare, 2 minutes for medium, 3 minutes for well done. Turn if additional browning is desired, judging time accordingly.

Do not fry too many pieces at a time when using grill. It is easier to turn pieces over for proper browning if there is space between them.

Do not overload the fryer basket in the "Fry All" as this will reduce the temperature of the hot oil and prevent it from searing food fast. Better to do a little at a time, as each batch takes only a few minutes.

Prepare accompanying sauces for fried and grilled food first. That way the fried food will be ready to eat as soon as it is cooked.

ABOUT THIS BOOK

Care has been taken to explain each step of preparing these recipes so that you may follow them with ease. It helps to read a recipe through completely before starting to prepare it, so you will be able to assemble the needed ingredients. A few words of additional explanation may be helpful.

Ingredients are listed in the order in which they should be used. At times directions are given to use part of an ingredient and then later use the remaining part for another step in the recipe.

Wherever butter, shortening, vegetable oil or any other fat has been specified you may substitute the type of your own choice.

Herbs are dried unless otherwise specified. If you can obtain fresh ones, do so. Multiply the dried quantity by two or three when using fresh herbs.

Occasionally a weight of ounces or pounds is given for a canned food. This is merely a guide. If other cans are within an ounce or part of an ounce, you may make a substitution.

Amounts are given for salt and pepper. As with all seasonings, these are approximate. You should taste and correct seasonings by adding enough to get the flavor you prefer.

A handy way to dredge food—that is, to coat it with flour—is to place flour in a paper or plastic bag and shake all or some of the food in it. When finished, it is easy to dispose of the bag without having any mess.

This cookbook should serve as a stimulus to your own creativity. Use the recipes and then make whatever substitutions for sandwich fillings and batter dippers you desire.

How To Use Your Fast Cooker

Before using your "Double Mac" or "Little Mac" fast cooker, read the directions for use and maintenance that come with it. File these instructions for handy reference as you learn to use the cooker in many ways.

HOW TO USE FOR CLOSED COOKING

1. Before using for the first time, wash the non-stick surfaces with hot sudsy water, using a soft sponge or dishcloth. Rinse thoroughly and dry, taking care not to immerse the top cover in water, as this contains the heating element.

2. Brush salad oil or melted unsalted shortening on surfaces for conditioning.

3. When ready to use, place desired side of cooking plate in the bottom tray: round for hamburgers or rectangular (square) for sandwiches and irregular pieces of meat and fish.

4. Place top cover on, inserting hinge securely.

5. Press handle lock into position.

6. Preheat unit for approximately 5 minutes.

7. Open and follow recipe directions before covering and locking as above. Cook for allotted time. Remove food. Unplug and cool the cooker. Clean and store.

HOW TO USE FOR OPEN GRILLING

1. Turn lid of "Double Mac" over and stand on its feet, forming a flat grill. Place top cover of "Little Mac" with heating element into bottom drip tray for support.

2. Preheat grill 3 to 5 minutes.

3. Add butter or oil as directed in recipe, letting butter melt before adding food.

4. Add desired food and cook as suggested in recipe.

HOW TO USE "FRY ALL"

1. Remove lid and add cooking oil or shortening.
2. Heat 5 minutes.
3. Add desired food to be deep fried. Fry until golden brown. Lift basket and hook drainage bracket on side of base, letting fried food drain.
4. Unplug and cool. Wipe around exterior to remove drips. Do not immerse in water. When cool, replace lid. Refrigerate food if desired.
5. After several uses, pour oil through a cheesecloth-lined strainer into a container, to remove breading and other residue from frying. Wipe out interior of fryer with paper toweling. Pour strained oil back into fryer, replace lid and store until next use.

HOW TO CLEAN FAST COOKERS

1. Do not immerse parts with heating elements in water. Instead, wipe around with a soft sudsy cloth and rinse with another. Then wipe dry.
2. Parts without heating elements may be immersed in sudsy water, rinsed and dried.
3. Always allow units to cool completely before cleaning. Unplug from outlet when not in use.

ABOUT BREAD

Often referred to as the "staff of life," bread has been an important source of nourishment since biblical times. But did you know that the bread we take for granted today was also employed as a medium of exchange, its abundance or scarcity revealing the wealth or impoverishment of early households?

Records show that the Egyptians knew, over 6,000 years ago, that fermented dough could rise and be baked to provide important sustenance for the daily diet. Workers and slaves were often paid for their labor with rations of bread instead of currency.

The Bible reveals that in the Exodus the Hebrews left Egypt so abruptly they were forced to take their unleavened dough with them, letting the sun bake it into flat sheets now called "matzohs." The Romans learned the art of baking bread too, and revealed this knowledge to the people they conquered, spreading the techniques far and wide.

Wheat was first brought to America from Europe by the early settlers, who planted the first grains in the New World. In turn, corn was taken back to Europe by early American explorers, becoming a staple source of flour and food in the Old World.

Now bread comes in all varieties of flour, natural or finely ground, and the ways to cook and serve it are a source of endless creativity.

This book will show you many nourishing things to do with bread. It can be dipped into a batter and served as French Toast, or filled as for a Croque, or toasted to await a juicy hamburger seasoned to your taste. Whichever you choose, you'll be following the basic nutritional tradition of serving grain with your meal.

ABOUT HAMBURGERS

Hamburgers are probably as American as apple pie. No one seems to know exactly where or when the idea originated to grind up beef and cook it rather than to serve it raw, as the Europeans serve "tartare."

Perhaps it all began at the 1893 World's Fair in St. Louis, as did the ice cream cone. Or maybe it is true that hamburgers were first served in New Haven to whatever Yale lambs had found their way to a local eatery. Or maybe the hamburger was a natural evolution of the need for an inexpensive meat dish to be served to the teeming hordes of workers in factories at the turn of the century.

Wherever the hamburger started, it has spread throughout the world as an American food invention. But no other country can prepare it as well as it is done here at home. We add seasonings and condiments to ground beef, top with cheese or onions, sometimes add lettuce and tomato, spread with catsup, and put it all in a toasted bun. The only limitation is that of your own imagination and the preference for eating it rare, medium or well done.

From toddlers to teenagers, from young people on a budget to retirees, it seems as if everyone in the country reaches for a satisfying hamburger several times a week.

With a "Mac" fast cooker, it is easy to provide this home-style cooking that everybody loves. Just mix up the beef to your taste, cook it in minutes and pop in into a round roll. Pass the catsup and watch the grins of contentment with the first bite.

Preheat with water approximately 6 minutes unless otherwise suggested. Cooking times are approximate and may depend on personal preference.

Cooking Method	Food and Amount	Cooking Times	Directions
To boil, cook and heat	Hot dogs (up to 10)	5-8 min. after water boils	Add to cold or hot water.
	Boil-in-bag foods (1 package)	As suggested on package	Place in 3 cups boiling water.
	Spaghetti (2 oz.)	8-12 minutes	Use 3 cups water. Follow package directions.
	Vegetables	Until desired doneness, depending on vegetable	Use 3 cups water to 2 cups vegetables. Place vegetables in cold water.
	Soups (ready-to serve can)	15-20 minutes	Place opened can in 3 cups water.
	Boiled eggs	Medium soft 3-4 minutes Hard boiled 15 minutes	Have unshelled eggs at room temperature. Place in "Fry All". Add cold water to cover tops by one inch. Pull plug after water has come to a rapid boil. Let stand for desired time. Cool promptly and thoroughly in cold water to make shells easier to remove.

COOKING PROCEDURE FOR "FRY ALL"

Add butter or margarine if desired. Cooking times are approximate and depend on personal preference.

DO NOT USE BASKET

Cooking Method	Food and Amount	Directions
Grilling	Hot dogs (5)	Do not preheat. Do not crowd. Turn for desired browning.
	Bacon—2 strips cut in two	Do not preheat. Turn as desired.
	Fried eggs (1)	Do not preheat. Cook to desired doneness. Prepare eggs as desired.
	Scrambled (2)	Do not preheat. When mixture begins to set, stir bottom and sides till eggs are cooked to suit personal taste.
	Omelette (2 eggs)	See recipe section.
	Sandwich (1)	Preheat "Fry All" approximately 6 minutes. Grill on both sides until brown as desired.
	French toast (1 slice bread)	Preheat "Fry All" approximately 6 minutes. Grill on both sides until browned as desired.
	Hamburgers (2)	Do not preheat. Grill on both sides until browned as desired. If meat is very fatty, hook basket in place to check spatter. Rare will take 5-6 minutes. Well done 8-10 minutes.
	Steaks (1) Cube or minute Small rib or sirloin	Do not preheat. Grill on both sides until browned as desired. If meat is very fatty, hook basket in place to check spatter. Cube or minute steak will take 1-2 minutes each side, rib or sirloin 3-5 minutes each side.

COOKING PROCEDURE FOR "FRY ALL"

Preheat approximately 6 minutes. Cooking times are approximate and may depend on personal preference.

Cooking Method	Food	Cooking Times
Deep frying	Potatoes	
	Frozen french fries	4-5 minutes
	Frozen shoe strings	5-6 minutes
	Raw fries	5-6 minutes
	Frozen onion rings	1-2 minutes
	Frozen French-fried shrimp	3-4 minutes
	Frozen zucchini or eggplant strips	3-4 minutes
	Frozen fish sticks	2-3 minutes
	Frozen fish fillets	2-3 minutes
	Fresh fish fillets	3-4 minutes
	Pre-cooked frozen chicken	4-5 minutes
	Frozen clams	30 seconds-1 minute
	Donuts (2 donuts, 4 holes)	1-2 minutes

Breakfast

There's no reason for breakfast to be boring, even if you are in a hurry. The fast cooker makes it possible to prepare in a matter of minutes a hot and hearty head start to your day. Nutritionists say that when you skip breakfast you'll suffer an energy lag by midmorning. Don't take the chance of having to depend on coffee-break junk food at work; start your day with a good meal that will sustain you all the way to lunch.

1 slice white bread [not thin] Dash salt
2 tablespoons butter   Dash pepper
1 egg

Leave the crust on the bread to help hold the shape of the hole. Cut a round piece from the center of the bread with a 2½" cookie cutter. Place top cover of "Double Mac" with open grill facing up. Heat for 5 minutes. Add 1 tablespoon of the butter; when melted, put on bread slice. Break egg into a cup and slide it carefully into hole in bread. Season with salt and pepper. Cook until egg is set and bread nicely browned on bottom, 3-4 minutes. Lift off Bird-In-The-Nest with spatula; add remaining butter to grill and flip over bread to brown second side, about 1 minute. Egg will be slightly runny; cook longer if you prefer.

Yield: 1 serving

Note: If using "Little Mac" place top cover with heating element into bottom drip tray.

BUTTERMILK PANCAKES

2 eggs, separated   ½ teaspoon sugar
1 cup buttermilk   ½ teaspoon salt
¾ cup flour   1 tablespoon peanut oil
¼ teaspoon baking soda   1 tablespoon butter
½ teaspoon baking powder

Beat egg yolks; mix with buttermilk. Stir in flour. Add remaining dry ingredients. Beat egg whites stiff and fold in. Heat open "Double Mac" grill 5 minutes. Add oil and butter. When butter melts, drop batter by spoonsful onto grill; cook until bubbles appear on top and bottoms are golden. Turn to brown other side. Repeat; add more oil and butter if needed. Leftover batter will keep a day or two in the refrigerator.

Yield: 2 servings

Note: If using "Little Mac" make one at a time.

BREADCRUMB PANCAKES

¾ cup milk
1 tablespoon butter
¼ cup fresh breadcrumbs
1 egg beaten
2 teaspoons baking powder

¼ cup flour
¼ teaspoon salt
½ teaspoon sugar
1 tablespoon butter

Scald milk; stir in butter and breadcrumbs. Let stand until breadcrumbs are soft. Add egg. Sift baking powder, flour, salt and sugar together; stir into mixture. Heat open "Double Mac" grill 5 minutes. Add butter; when melted, make pancakes, adding more butter if necessary. Repeat.
Yield: 2 servings
Note: If using "Little Mac," make one at a time.

OATMEAL PANCAKES

1 cup milk
¾ cup oatmeal, quick or
    old fashioned, uncooked
½ cup flour, sifted
1¼ teaspoons baking powder

½ teaspoon salt
1 tablespoon sugar
1 egg, beaten
2½ tablespoons melted butter
Butter

Pour milk over oatmeal and let stand. Sift together flour, baking powder, salt and sugar. Stir egg into milk-oatmeal mixture. Add sifted dry ingredients and stir in the melted butter. Heat open "Double Mac" grill 5 minutes. Butter it lightly. Fry pancakes on grill until brown on bottom and showing bubbles on top. Turn and brown second side, adding more butter if necessary. Repeat. Serve with jam or preserves, if desired.
Yield: 2 servings
Note: If using "Little Mac" make one at a time.

2 cups flour	2 eggs
3 teaspoons baking powder	1⅓ cups milk
1 teaspoon salt	2 tablespoons melted shortening
1 tablespoon sugar	1 cup fresh blueberries

Mix and sift dry ingredients. Beat eggs well; add milk. Add dry mixture; beat until smooth. Add shortening and berries; mix well. Heat open "Double Mac" grill 5 minutes. Drop pancake mixture by tablespoons on lightly greased grill. Cook on first side until bubbles appear on top. Turn and brown on second side, 1-2 minutes. Repeat. Serve with melted butter and heated maple syrup. Leftover batter may be kept in the refrigerator up to two days.

Yield: 2 dozen small pancakes

Note: If using "Little Mac" cook two at a time, spreading batter into oval shape.

BREAKFAST PANCAKES

1½ cups flour	2 tablespoons shortening
2 teaspoons baking powder	1½ cups milk
½ cup white cornmeal	1 egg, slightly beaten
¼ teaspoon salt	

Combine dry ingredients. Cut in shortening. Add milk and egg; mix well. Heat open "Double Mac" grill 5 minutes. Grease it lightly. Drop batter by spoonsful; cook until bubbles appear on surface, about 2 minutes. Turn and brown second side. Grease grill lightly and repeat. Leftover batter may be kept in refrigerator for use next day.

Yield: 1 dozen large pancakes

Note: If using "Little Mac" cook one at a time. Serve with melted butter and heated maple syrup or honey, if desired. Defrosted precooked sausages, well browned, or crisp bacon, are good accompaniments.

1 7½-ounce can minced clams	¾ cup clam liquor and milk
¾ cup sifted flour	1 egg, beaten
½ cup yellow cornmeal	Butter
2½ teaspoons baking powder	Cran-Applesauce [see below]
½ teaspoon salt	

Drain clams, reserving liquor. Sift dry ingredients together. Add milk to clam liquor to measure ¾ cup. Add to dry ingredients; stir only until blended. Heat open "Double Mac" grill 5 minutes. Butter it well. Spoon out enough batter to make 2 pancakes at a time. Cook until brown on the bottom and bubbles appear on top surface, 1-2 minutes. Turn, adding more butter if needed, and brown second side. Repeat.

Yield: 9 pancakes

Note: If using "Little Mac" cook one at a time.

CRAN-APPLESAUCE

1 1-pound can jellied cranberry sauce	½ cup applesauce
	¼ teaspoon cinnamon

Combine all ingredients and blend thoroughly. Chill.

Yield: 2½ cups sauce

2 cups water

1 teaspoon salt

½ cup cornmeal

½ cup minced cooked ham

Flour

1 tablespoon vegetable oil

1 tablespoon butter

Prepare polenta the day before you plan to use it. Bring water to a boil; add salt. Slowly stir in cornmeal and continue stirring so it will not form lumps. Bring to a boil again, being careful to see that it does not boil over. Boil 5 minutes. Transfer to the top of a double boiler and continue cooking over hot water for ½ hour. Stir in ham and mix thoroughly. Pour into a square pan; chill overnight. Cut into 3" x 1" slices. Dredge with flour. Heat open "Double Mac" grill 5 minutes. Add oil and butter; when butter is melted, add polenta. Cook until brown and crisp on all sides, 3 to 4 minutes. Repeat.

Yield: 2 servings

Note: If using "Little Mac" cook one slice at a time.

FRENCH TOAST

1 egg

1 cup milk

¼ teaspoon cinnamon

1 teaspoon sugar

4 slices white bread

Butter

Beat egg and milk together with cinnamon and sugar. Soak bread slices in this mixture until all is absorbed. Turn occasionally while soaking. Heat open "Double Mac" grill 5 minutes. Butter it well. Add two pieces of soaked bread and saute until golden brown, 2 to 3 minutes. Turn and brown other side, adding more butter if needed. Repeat.

Yield: 4 slices

Note: If using "Little Mac" cook one at a time. Serve with melted butter and hot maple syrup or honey, if desired.

SALMON SCRAPPLE

Real Philadelphia scrapple is one of the best things to eat for breakfast. Here's a tasty variation that includes salmon for extra protein.

1 cup water
⅓ cup yellow cornmeal
¼ teaspoon salt

⅓ cup cold water
⅔ cup flaked salmon
2 tablespoons peanut oil

Bring the cup of water to a boil. Mix cornmeal and salt with the cold water and gradually add to boiling water, stirring to prevent lumps. Cook until thickened, stirring constantly. Cover and cook over low heat 10 minutes, stirring occasionally. Add salmon and mix well. Pour into a loaf pan. Cool. Refrigerate overnight, covered. To cook, slice about ¾" thick. Heat open "Double Mac" grill 5 minutes. Add 2 tablespoons peanut oil. Put in slices of scrapple and cook until browned on one side, 2 to 3 minutes. Turn, adding more oil if needed, and brown second side. Repeat.
Yield: 2 servings

FRIED APPLE RINGS

1 MacIntosh apple
1 tablespoon lemon juice
3 tablespoons brown sugar
2 tablespoons sherry

1 tablespoon vegetable oil
1 tablespoon butter
Cinnamon-Sugar

Core apple. Cut in half and cut each half into 4 even slices. Put into a bowl with lemon juice, sugar and sherry; allow to marinate for 20 minutes. Drain apple slices and dip in flour. Heat open "Double Mac" grill for 5 minutes. Add oil and butter; when butter melts, put in some apple slices. Cook, turning frequently, until they are lightly brown and slightly soft, 2 to 3 minutes. Repeat. Sprinkle with cinnamon-sugar.
Yield: 2 servings
Note: If using "Little Mac" cook one at a time. This is a good accompaniment to sausage cakes.

¾ cup quick-cooking oatmeal	Butter
1½ cups boiling water	Honey
½ teaspoon salt	

Stir oatmeal into briskly boiling salted water. Cook 1 minute, stirring occasionally. Cover pan, remove from heat and let stand a few minutes. Pour into a loaf pan. Cool slightly and refrigerate several hours or overnight. Cut into slices. Dredge lightly with flour. Heat open "Double Mac" grill 5 minutes. Add 1 tablespoon butter; melt. Put on oatmeal slices and cook until browned on bottom, 2 to 3 minutes. Turn and brown second side. Repeat. Serve with honey.

Yield: 2 servings

Note: If using "Little Mac" cook one slice at a time. Bacon is a good addition to this.

FRIED MUSH

⅓ cup cornmeal	1 cup boiling water
¼ teaspoon salt	Butter
⅓ cup cold water	Hot maple syrup

Combine cornmeal, salt and cold water. Pour into boiling water, stirring rapidly. Bring to boil, stirring constantly. Lower heat; cover and cook 10 minutes, stirring occasionally. Pour into a loaf pan rinsed with cold water. Cool; cover and refrigerate several hours or overnight. Cut into slices. Heat open "Double Mac" grill 5 minutes. Melt 1 tablespoon butter on it. Add mush slices and cook until golden on bottom. Turn, adding more butter if needed, and brown second side. Repeat. Serve with heated maple syrup.

Yield: 2 servings

Note: If using "Little Mac" cook one at a time. Fried ham steak is good with this.

Sandwiches

Ever since the Earl of Sandwich ordered his meal to be placed between two slices of bread so he could eat his dinner without interrupting a game of cards, people have been inventing ingenious fillings for the sandwiches named after him. They have become a steady item in the American diet, hot or cold, and for all meals. The fast cooker makes it possible for you to prepare sandwiches with very little muss and fuss. It's easy when you have a "Mac" working for you.

2 tablespoons butter, softened
1 teaspoon Worcestershire sauce
4 slices thin white bread
4 slices Swiss cheese
2 slices boiled ham

1 egg, lightly beaten
2 tablespoons milk
Dash salt
Butter

Mix butter with ½ teaspoon of the Worcestershire sauce until well blended. Spread on one side of each slice of bread. Top two slices of the bread with a slice of Swiss cheese, a slice of ham and another slice of cheese. Place remaining bread slices, butter side down, on top. Mix egg with milk, salt and remaining ½ teaspoon of Worcestershire sauce. Dip each side of each sandwich into egg mixture. Heat open "Double Mac" grill 5 minutes. Butter it well. Place sandwiches on it and cook about 2 minutes, or until bottoms are golden. Turn, adding more butter if needed, and brown second side.

Yield: 2 servings

Note: If using "Little Mac" cook one at a time.

HAM LOAF SANDWICH

4 slices whole wheat bread
Sliced ham loaf [see page 25]

Butter

Cut ham loaf into ¼" thick slices, in a shape to fit bread. Place slices of loaf on two bread slices. Cover with other two slices. Heat open "Double Mac" grill 5 minutes, butter generously and place sandwiches on it. Butter the tops of sandwiches. Cook until bottoms are browned, about 2 minutes. Turn and brown second side for about 1 minute.

Yield: 2 servings

Note: If using "Little Mac" cook one at a time.

½ cup chicken, minced fine
¼ cup celery, minced fine
1/8 teaspoon salt
Dash freshly ground pepper

2 tablespoons mayonnaise
4 very thin slices ham
4 slices oatmeal bread
Butter

Mix chicken and celery. Season with salt and pepper. Mix with mayonnaise. Place a slice of ham on each of two slices of bread. Top each with half the chicken mixture, then with another slice of ham. Cover with remaining two bread slices. Heat open "Double Mac" grill 5 minutes. Melt butter on grill; add sandwiches. Butter the top sides of the sandwiches. Cook until the bottom is golden brown, about 2 minutes. Turn and brown the other side to golden.

Yield: 2 servings

Note: If using "Little Mac" cook one at a time.

HAM LOAF

1¼ pounds smoked ham
1¼ pounds fresh pork
¾ cup plus 2 tablespoons
    cracker meal

¾ cup plus 2 tablespoons milk
2 eggs, well beaten
10 tablespoons catsup
5 tablespoons brown sugar

Grind the ham and pork fine. Mix with cracker meal, milk, eggs and 5 tablespoons of the catsup. Pack lightly into a loaf pan and bake in 375°F. oven 30 minutes. Mix brown sugar with remaining 5 tablespoons catsup and spread over the top of the loaf. Continue baking for another 30 minutes.

Yield: 4-5 servings

1 3-ounce package cream cheese
1 2¼-ounce can deviled ham
½ teaspoon chili powder
¼ teaspoon Dijon mustard

Dash freshly ground pepper
6 slices sprouted wheat bread
Butter

Preheat "Double Mac" for 5 minutes. Thoroughly mix all ingredients except bread and butter. Spread on three bread slices. Cover with remaining bread slices. Place two sandwiches in Mac; butter tops. Close lid and lock handle. Cook 2 minutes. Turn, butter tops; cook 1 minute longer, or until browned to your taste. Repeat with remaining sandwiches.

Yield: 3 servings

Note: If using "Little Mac" cook one at a time. Extra filling refrigerates well for several days if one 1 or 2 servings are desired.

DEVILED HAM AND APPLE SANDWICH

1 2¼-ounce can deviled ham
¼ cup finely chopped apple
1 tablespoon mayonnaise
½ teaspoon prepared mustard

4 slices rye bread
6 thin slices cucumber
Butter

Mix ham, apple, mayonnaise and mustard well. Spread two bread slices with mixture. Top each with three slices of cucumber. Top with remaining bread slices. Heat open "Double Mac" grill for 5 minutes. Melt butter on it. Add sandwiches and cook until golden brown on bottom. Turn and brown second side, adding more butter if necessary.

Yield: 2 servings

Note: If using "Little Mac" cook one at a time.

¼ cup mayonnaise
2 teaspoons chopped chutney
1 teaspoon curry powder
1/8 teaspoon salt
1 cup shredded cabbage

4 slices rye bread
⅓ pound baked ham, sliced very thin
2 slices Cheddar cheese
Butter

Combine mayonnaise, chutney, curry powder, salt and cabbage. On each of 2 slices of bread place equal quantities of sliced ham, half of the cabbage mixture and 1 slice of cheese. Top with remaining bread. Heat open "Double Mac" grill 5 minutes. Melt 1 tablespoon butter and add sandwiches. Cook on first side until golden brown, 2-3 minutes. Turn and brown second side, adding butter if needed.

Yield: 2 servings

Note: If using "Little Mac" cook one at a time.

HAM SALAD SANDWICH

1 cup finely chopped cooked ham
2 tablespoons shredded carrot
1 tablespoon finely chopped dill pickle
1 tablespoon finely chopped onion
¼ cup mayonnaise

1 teaspoon Worcestershire sauce
Dash garlic powder
4 slices rye bread with seeds
Butter

Mix all ingredients except bread and butter thoroughly. Spread on two of the bread slices. Cover with remaining slices. Heat "Double Mac" 5 minutes. Add sandwiches; butter tops. Cover and cook until one side is browned, about 2 minutes. Turn, butter tops, cover and brown second side.

Yield: 2 servings

Note: If using "Little Mac" cook one at a time.

¼ cup butter
1 teaspoon Dijon mustard
1 teaspoon chopped parsley
½ cup chopped cooked chicken
¼ cup well-drained chopped
    pineapple

1/8 teaspoon salt
Dash freshly ground pepper
1 tablespoon mayonnaise
4 slices protein bread
Butter

Cream ¼ cup butter with mustard, parsley, chicken and pineapple. Add salt and pepper. Mix in mayonnaise. Spread on two slices of bread. Top with remaining slices. Heat open "Double Mac" grill 5 minutes. Grease it lightly. Place sandwiches on grill and cook until bread is lightly toasted on the bottom, about 2 minutes. Turn and toast second side.

Yield: Makes 2 servings
Note: If using "Little Mac" cook one at a time.

2 tablespoons butter
¼ cup grated Cheddar cheese
¼ cup ground boiled ham
1 teaspoon half-and-half cream

¼ teaspoon soy sauce
Dash Tabasco
4 slices rye bread
Butter

Mix all ingredients except the bread and butter. Spread on two slices of bread. Top with remaining slices. Heat "Double Mac" 5 minutes. Add sandwiches; butter tops. Cover and cook until nicely brown, about 2 minutes. Turn, butter tops; cover and brown second side.

Yield: 2 servings
Note: If using "Little Mac" cook one at a time.

4 thin slices Swiss cheese
2 thin slices cooked ham

4 slices white bread
Butter

Place one slice of Swiss cheese, a thin slice of ham and another slice of cheese (all cut to fit the bread size) on each of two slices of bread. Top with remaining bread slices. Heat "Double Mac" for 5 minutes. Add Croques. Butter tops; cover and cook about 3 minutes, or until golden brown. Turn, butter tops, cover and brown other side, about 1 minute.

Yield: 2 servings

Note: If using "Little Mac" cook one at a time. For variety substitute a thin slice of blue cheese for one of the Swiss cheese slices in each sandwich. To make a Croque Madame: substitute chicken for the ham used above.

FRENCH TOASTED HAM SANDWICH

¾ cup minced cooked ham
2 tablespoons mayonnaise
1 teaspoon prepared mustard
4 slices white bread

½ cup milk
1 egg, slightly beaten
Butter

Mix ham with mayonnaise and mustard. Spread on two slices of bread. Top with remaining slices. Heat open "Double Mac" grill 5 minutes. Add butter and melt. Mix milk and egg; dip sandwiches into mixture to coat well. Place on grill and saute until golden on bottom, about 2 minutes. Turn, adding butter if necessary, and brown the other side.

Yield: 2 servings

Note: If using "Little Mac" cook one at a time.

Here's a tiny meat loaf that will provide a dinner for two and leftovers for sandwiches. Any way you eat it, it's a tasty combination.

BABY MEAT LOAF

½ **pound chopped chuck**
3 tablespoons chopped onion
2 tablespoons chopped green pepper
1 egg
Dash garlic powder

¼ **teaspoon salt**
1/8 teaspoon freshly ground pepper
⅓ **cup Italian seasoned breadcrumbs**
½ **cup tomato catsup**

Mix all ingredients except catsup and press into a 5¾" x 3¼" x 2¼" loaf pan. Bake in 350°F. oven 30 minutes. Pour catsup over and bake 30 minutes longer.
Yield: 2 servings plus leftovers

MEAT LOAF SANDWICH

4 slices rye bread
4 thin slices meat loaf

Butter

Place meat loaf, cut about ¼" thick, on two bread slices. Carefully spread the catsup which has been cooked on top of the loaf, over the slice, so that it won't leak out while cooking. Cover with remaining two slices of bread. Heat open "Double Mac" grill 5 minutes. Melt butter on it. Put sandwiches on grill; butter tops. Cook until browned on bottom, about 2 minutes. Turn and brown second side for 1 minute.
Yield: 2 servings
Note: If using "Little Mac" cook one at a time.

¼ cup grated sharp Cheddar cheese
2 tablespoons mayonnaise
⅔ cup shredded corned beef
2 tablespoons pickle relish
1 tablespoon grated onion
2 tablespoons minced parsley

1/8 teaspoon salt
1/8 teaspoon paprika
1/8 teaspoon curry powder
½ teaspoon Worcestershire sauce
4 slices rye bread
Butter

Beat cheese and mayonnaise together. Add corned beef. Mix well; add remaining ingredients, except bread and butter. Spread on two slices of the bread. Cover with remaining slices. Heat open "Double Mac" grill 5 minutes. Add 1 tablespoon butter and place sandwiches on grill. Cook until bottoms are golden brown, about 2 minutes. Turn, adding more butter if needed; cook until brown on second side.

Yield: 2 servings

Note: If using "Little Mac" cook one at a time.

HOT PASTRAMI SANDWICH

4 slices pumpernickel or rye bread
¼ pound hot pastrami, thinly sliced

Butter
Mustard

Place pastrami on two slices of bread. Cover with the other two slices. Heat open "Double Mac" grill 5 minutes. Add butter; melt. Cook sandwiches until browned on one side, about 2 minutes. Turn, add more butter and brown the other side. Serve mustard on the side.

Yield: 2 servings

Note: Heat pastrami in a double boiler before assembling sandwiches. If using "Little Mac" cook one at a time.

1 cup finely ground cooked tongue
1 tablespoon pickle relish
1 tablespoon chopped chives
1 hard-cooked egg, chopped

1 teaspoon prepared mustard
6 slices rye bread
Butter

Mix all ingredients except bread and butter. Spread on three slices of the bread. Heat open "Double Mac" grill 5 minutes. Butter it lightly and place two sandwiches on it. Butter top sides. Cook until browned to your taste on bottom, about 2 minutes. Turn and brown the second side. Cook the third in the same way (or wrap third sandwich in plastic wrap and refrigerate for future use).
Yield: 3 servings
Note: If using "Little Mac" cook one at a time.

4 slices rye bread
4 thin square slices Muenster cheese
8 thin slices corned beef

¼ cup drained sauerkraut
4 thin slices cooked chicken
Butter

Cover each of two bread slices with 2 cheese slices, 4 slices corned beef and 2 tablespoons sauerkraut. Top each with 2 slices chicken and cover with remaining bread slices. Spread top side of sandwiches with butter. Heat "Double Mac" 5 minutes. Put on sandwiches, cover unhinged, and cook until golden, about 2 minutes. Turn, butter tops and cover and cook 1 minute, or until browned.
Yield: 2 servings
Note: If using "Little Mac" cook one at a time.

1 hard-cooked egg, shelled
¼ pound chicken livers, cooked
2 medium mushrooms, chopped
1 tablespoon minced onion
1 tablespoon butter

1 tablespoon mayonnaise
1/8 teaspoon salt
Dash freshly ground pepper, to taste
4 slices rye bread
Butter

Chop egg and chicken livers together. In a skillet, saute mushrooms and onion together 5 minutes in 1 tablespoon butter. Mix all together; add salt and pepper. Spread half the mixture on each of two slices of bread. Top with remaining slices. Heat open "Double Mac" grill 5 minutes. Melt butter on it. Add sandwiches and cook 2 minutes, or until golden brown on the bottom. Turn, adding more butter if necessary, and brown second side.

Yield: 2 servings
Note: If using "Little Mac" cook one at a time.

CHICKEN AND ALMOND SANDWICH

⅓ cup minced cooked chicken
⅓ cup minced blanched almonds
1 tablespoon mayonnaise
¼ teaspoon salt

Dash freshly ground pepper
4 slices white bread
Butter

Mix chicken, almonds and mayonnaise. Add salt and pepper; spread half of mixture on each of two slices of bread. Cover with remaining slices. Heat open "Double Mac" grill 5 minutes. Melt 1 tablespoon butter on it; place sandwiches on top. Cook about 2 minutes, or until golden. Turn, adding more butter if needed, and cook until second side is golden.

Yield: 2 servings
Note: If using "Little Mac" cook one at a time.

LUSCIOUS CHICKEN SANDWICH

½ cup finely chopped
   cooked chicken
2 tablespoons finely chopped celery
1 tablespoon finely chopped
   pitted ripe olives
1½ tablespoons chopped onion
1½ tablespoons chopped pimiento

3 tablespoons sour cream
½ teaspoon lemon juice
¼ teaspoon Worcestershire sauce
¼ teaspoon salt
4 slices very thin white bread
Butter

Combine chicken, celery, olives and pimiento. Mix sour cream, lemon juice, Worcestershire and salt. Stir into chicken mixture and blend well. Spread on two slices of bread. Top with remaining slices. Heat "Double Mac" 5 minutes. Butter top slices. Cover and cook 2 minutes, or until golden brown. Turn and butter tops; cover and brown other sides, about 1½ minutes.

Yield: 2 servings

Note: If using "Little Mac" cook one at a time.

SPECIAL CHICKEN SANDWICH

4 slices white bread
4 slices cooked chicken
4 slices crisp bacon

4 tablespoons grated Swiss cheese
Butter
Mushroom Sauce [page 90], optional

Place 2 chicken slices on each of two slices of bread. Place bacon slices on top and sprinkle each with 2 tablespoons cheese. Cover with remaining bread slices. Heat "Double Mac" 5 minutes. Put on sandwiches; butter tops. Cover and cook until golden, 1-1½ minutes. Turn, butter tops; cover and cook until golden. Pour Mushroom Sauce over each sandwich, if desired.

Yield: 2 servings

Note: If using "Little Mac" cook one at a time.

1 3¼-ounce can salmon
2 tablespoons mayonnaise
½ teaspoon grated onion
1/8 teaspoon salt
Dash freshly ground pepper

4 slices bread
1 egg
1 tablespoon milk
Butter

Drain salmon, reserving liquid. Remove bones and flake the fish. Mix with mayonnaise and grated onion; season with salt and pepper. Spread mixture on two of the bread slices; cover with remaining slices. Beat egg; add milk and salmon liquid to it. Dip sandwiches in this mixture to coat both sides. Heat open "Double Mac" grill 5 minutes. Add 1 tablespoon butter and let it melt. Place sandwiches on grill. Cook until golden brown on bottom, 1-2 minutes. Turn and brown other side, adding more butter if needed.

Yield: 2 servings
Note: If using "Little Mac" cook one at a time.

4 slices Italian round loaf bread
Cream cheese
¼ pound smoked salmon, sliced thin

Very thin slices red onion
Butter

Spread 2 slices of the bread with cream cheese. Add half the salmon slices and then the onion slices. Top with remaining two slices of bread. Heat open "Double Mac" grill for 5 minutes. Add butter; and when melted, put on sandwiches. Butter top sides. Cook until bread is golden on bottom; about 1 minute. Turn and brown the other side.

Yield: 2 servings
Note: If using "Little Mac" cook one at a time.

1 hard-cooked egg, shelled
    and finely chopped
1 3¼-ounce can salmon, drained
    and flaked
2 tablespoons finely chopped celery
2 tablespoons mayonnaise
1 tablespoon finely chopped onion

1 teaspoon sweet pickle relish
1 teaspoon Worcestershire sauce
½ teaspoon lemon juice
Dash salt
Dash freshly ground pepper
4 slices pumpernickel bread
Butter

Thoroughly mix all ingredients except bread and butter. Spread on two slices of bread. Heat "Double Mac" 5 minutes. Put on sandwiches; spread butter on tops. Cover and cook 2 minutes. Turn; butter tops and cook 1½ minutes on the second side.

Yield: 2 servings
Note: If using "Little Mac" cook one at a time.

SPECIAL TUNA SANDWICH

4 canned Chinese water chestnuts
1 3½-ounce can white tuna, drained
2 tablespoons mayonnaise

Dash salt
4 slices white bread
Butter

Heat "Double Mac" 5 minutes. Cut water chestnuts into slices. Mix with tuna, mayonnaise and salt. Spread tuna mixture on two bread slices. Top with remaining slices. Place sandwiches on grill; butter tops. Cover and cook until golden, about 2 minutes. Turn, butter top; cover and cook until other side is golden.

Yield: 2 servings
Note: If using "Little Mac" cook one at a time.

1 3½-ounce can tuna
1 hard-cooked egg, shelled
2 tablespoons mayonnaise
1/8 teaspoon salt

Dash freshly ground pepper
1/8 teaspoon basil
4 slices whole wheat bread
Butter

Flake tuna. Chop egg coarsely. Mix all ingredients but bread and butter. Spread on two slices of bread. Top with remaining slices. Heat open "Double Mac" grill 5 minutes. Butter it lightly. Put on sandwiches; cook 2 minutes. Turn, adding a little more butter, and cook another 2 minutes.

Yield: 2 servings

Note: If using "Little Mac" cook one at a time.

1 3¾-ounce can skinless and
    boneless sardines
1 tablespoon chopped, stuffed
    green olives
1 tablespoon half-and-half cream

2 teaspoons lemon juice
1½ teaspoons Worcestershire sauce
1 teaspoon onion powder
4 slices protein bread
Butter

Mash sardines. Add remaining ingredients, except bread and butter, and mix well. Spread half of mixture on each of two slices of bread. Cover with remaining slices. Heat "Double Mac" 5 minutes. Put on sandwiches; butter tops. Cover and cook about 2 minutes. Turn, butter tops; cover and brown second side.

Yield: 2 servings

Note: If using "Little Mac" cook one at a time.

1 3¼-ounce can skinless and
    boneless sardines
1 tablespoon minced onion
1 teaspoon lemon juice

2 tablespoons mayonnaise
4 slices very thin white bread
Butter

Mash sardines well. Mix with onion, lemon juice and mayonnaise. Spread on two slices of bread. Top with remaining slices. Heat open "Double Mac" grill 5 minutes. Melt butter on it; add sandwiches. Cook until golden brown on bottom. Turn, adding more butter if needed, and brown second side.
Yield: 2 servings
Note: If using "Little Mac" cook one at a time.

¾ cup flaked crabmeat
½ cup chopped cucumber
¼ teaspoon Worcestershire sauce
2 tablespoons mayonnaise

6 slices white bread
½ cup shredded Cheddar cheese
Butter

Combine crabmeat, cucumber, Worcestershire sauce and mayonnaise. Spread three slices of bread with the mixture. Sprinkle with cheese. Top with remaining bread slices. Heat open "Double Mac" grill 5 minutes. Butter it well. Put on two of the sandwiches and cook until golden on the bottom, about 2 minutes. Turn, adding more butter if necessary, and brown other side. Remove from grill and cook third sandwich the same way.
Yield: 3 servings
Note: If using "Little Mac" cook one at a time.

Balachaung is served in Rangoon, Burma, with curries. Leftovers make tasty sandwich fillings with unusual flair.

¼ cup peanut oil
2 cloves garlic, peeled and sliced
2 small dried red chilis, crushed

Dash of turmeric
1 tablespoon vinegar
1 pound dry prawns,* crushed
    in the blender

Heat open "Double Mac" grill 5 minutes. Add oil; when hot, add sliced garlic and fry until light brown, about 1 minute. Remove garlic and drain on paper toweling. Add crushed chilis and the turmeric and cook 1 minute. Add crushed prawns and fry until oil is almost entirely absorbed, stirring occasionally, about 1 minute. Remove from grill and stir in the garlic slices.
Yield: About ½ cup
Note: If using "Little Mac" cook half at a time.
* Obtainable in Oriental food stores

TO MAKE A BALACHAUNG SANDWICH: Cool and clean Mac grill. Spread Balachaung on a slice of bread and cover with another slice. Heat Mac grill 5 minutes; add butter. Put on sandwich and cook 2 minutes to brown first side. Turn and brown second side, about 1 minute.
Yield: 1 serving

DATE-NUT BREAD SANDWICH

4 tablespoons cream cheese,
    at room temperature

4 slices date-nut bread
Butter

Heat open "Double Mac" grill 5 minutes. Spread cream cheese on two slices of bread. Top with remaining bread. Add butter to grill; when it melts, add sandwiches and cook until lightly browned on one side, about 2 minutes. Turn and brown second side, adding more butter if necessary.
Yield: 2 servings
Note: If using "Little Mac" cook one at a time.

4 slices thinly sliced Italian bread
4 slices Mozzarella cheese,
    sliced ¼ " thick
Anchovy paste
2 eggs, beaten

Dash salt
Dash freshly ground pepper
1 tablespoon olive oil
1 tablespoon butter

Place sliced cheese on two slices of bread. On other two slices, spread anchovy paste lightly. Put sandwiches together. Mix eggs with salt and pepper; soak sandwiches in this mixture for 20 minutes, until egg is absorbed, turning once. Heat open "Double Mac" grill 5 minutes. Add olive oil and butter; when butter melts, put on sandwiches. Cook until bottoms are golden brown, about 1 minute. Turn and cook other side until golden, adding a little more butter if necessary.

Yield: 2 servings
Note: If using "Little Mac" cook one at a time.

DRUMMER SANDWICH

1 3-ounce package cream cheese
1 tablespoon mayonnaise
¼ cup chopped walnuts

4 slices protein bread
Butter

Beat cheese and mayonnaise together until fluffy. Stir in nuts. Spread on two slices of bread. Top with remaining slices. Heat open "Double Mac" grill 5 minutes. Butter it lightly. Put on sandwiches and cook until golden on the bottom, about 2 minutes. Turn, adding a little more butter, and cook until second side is golden.

Yield: 2 servings
Note: If using "Little Mac" cook one at a time.

2 tablespoons mayonnaise
4 thin onion rings
¼ cup chopped green pepper
2 tablespoons butter
⅓ cup chili sauce

2 thin slices Cheddar cheese
    cut to fit bread
4 slices very thin white bread
Butter

Spread mayonnaise on two slices of bread. Cover each with two onion rings. In a skillet, cook green pepper in 2 tablespoons butter for 5 minutes; add chili sauce and stir. Spread over the onion rings. Add cheese slices and cover with remaining bread slices. Heat open "Double Mac" grill 5 minutes. Melt butter on it and add the sandwiches. Cook until golden on bottom, about 2 minutes. Turn and brown second side, adding more butter if necessary.

Yield: 2 servings

Note: If using "Little Mac" cook one at a time.

CREAM CHEESE AND CHUTNEY SANDWICH

1 3-ounce package cream cheese
1 teaspoon curry powder
2 teaspoons finely minced chutney

4 slices thinly sliced white bread
Butter

Preheat "Double Mac" for 5 minutes. Meanwhile, mix cheese, curry powder and chutney. Spread mixture on 2 slices of bread; top with remaining bread. Place on "Mac". Butter tops. Close lid and lock handle. Cook 2 minutes (check to see whether it is browned to your taste). Turn sandwich, butter and cook about 1 minute more.

Yield: 2 servings

Note: If using "Little Mac" cook one at a time. Extra filling refrigerates well for several days.

¼ pound blue cheese, mashed
1 tablespoon half-and-half cream
4 thin slices sweet red onion

2 tablespoons tomato catsup
4 slices pumpernickel
Butter

Mix mashed cheese with the half-and-half. Spread on 2 slices of pumpernickel. Place two slices of onion on each sandwich, then a tablespoon of catsup. Cover with remaining slices of pumpernickel. Heat open "Double Mac" grill 5 minutes. Melt 1 tablespoon butter on it. Put on sandwiches and cook to brown bottom side, about 3 minutes. Meanwhile, butter top side of sandwiches. Turn and brown second side, about 2 minutes.

Yield: 2 servings

Note: If using "Little Mac" cook one at a time.

4 slices oatmeal bread
2 slices Cheddar or Swiss cheese
Dijon mustard

4 slices crisp bacon
Sliced stuffed olives
Butter

Place a slice of cheese on each of two slices of bread. Spread with mustard to taste. Place two bacon slices, halved if necessary, on each sandwich base and add a few slices of olive. Top with remaining bread slices. Heat "Double Mac" 5 minutes. Place the sandwiches on it; butter tops. Cover and cook until brown, about 2 minutes. Turn, butter tops; cover and brown second side.

Yield: 2 servings

Note: If using "Little Mac" cook one at a time.

2 hard-cooked eggs	4 medium-sized mushrooms
1/8 teaspoon salt	2 tablespoons vegetable oil
Dash pepper	2 tablespoons butter
2 tablespoons mayonnaise	4 slices white bread

Shell and mash eggs with a fork. Season with salt and pepper. Mix in mayonnaise. Chop mushrooms coarsely. Heat open "Double Mac" grill 5 minutes. Add oil and butter; when butter melts, put in mushrooms. Cook, stirring occasionally, for 2 minutes. Remove mushroom pieces with slotted spoon, leaving fat in grill. Add mushrooms to eggs and mix well. Spread on two bread slices. Cover with remaining slices. Place sandwiches on grill and cook about 1 minute on first side, or until golden brown. Turn, adding butter if necessary, and brown second side of sandwiches.

Yield: 2 servings
Note: If using "Little Mac" cook one at a time.

2 hard-cooked eggs	½ teaspoon Worcestershire sauce
½ teaspoon Dijon mustard	1 tablespoon minced parsley
1 tablespoon pickle relish	4 slices thin white bread
1/8 teaspoon salt	Butter
Dash freshly ground pepper	

Shell eggs and chop as fine as possible (or push through a fine sieve). Mix with mustard, relish, salt, pepper, Worcestershire sauce and parsley. Spread on two slices of bread. Cover with remaining slices. Heat open "Double Mac" grill 5 minutes. Butter it well. Place sandwiches on grill and butter tops. When undersides are brown, about 2 minutes, turn and brown the other side.

Yield: 2 servings
Note: If using "Little Mac" cook one at a time.

1 cup baked beans   Butter
4 slices Boston brown bread

Spread baked beans on two slices of bread. Top with remaining slices. Heat open "Double Mac" grill 5 minutes. Add sandwiches. Butter tops of sandwiches. Cover and cook until browned to your taste, about 2 minutes. Turn, butter tops, cover and brown second side.
Yield: 2 servings

Here's how to make canned baked beans tastier:

1 1-pound can Boston baked   ¼ teaspoon dry mustard
   beans with pork   1 teaspoon Worcestershire sauce
1 small onion, minced   1½ tablespoons maple syrup
1 teaspoon bacon fat   2 slices bacon

Fry onion in bacon fat until well browned. Add beans, mustard, Worcestershire sauce and syrup; mix well, being careful not to break up pork. Place beans in a casserole with bacon slices on top. Bake in 400°F. oven 30 minutes. If bacon is not crisp at that point, broil for several minutes.
Yield: 4 servings

4 slices dark pumpernickel bread   4 slices bacon, cooked crisp
4 tablespoons peanut butter   and crumbled

Mix the bacon and peanut butter thoroughly; spread on two slices of bread. Cover with remaining slices. Heat "Double Mac" 5 minutes. Place sandwiches on ungreased square form and cover. Cook 4 minutes. Turn, cover and cook 3 minutes on other side.
Yield: 2 servings
Note: If using "Little Mac" cook one at a time.

This is often served by the Chinese, especially around Shanghai. It is really an Oriental salad, but it makes a most refreshing sandwich because Mac's speedy cooking of the bread allows the rest of the ingredients to remain crisp and cool on the inside.

½ **pound bean sprouts**	¾ **teaspoon vinegar**
1 quart boiling water	**1 teaspoon sugar**
¼ **cup shredded ham**	½ **teaspoon sesame oil,* optional**
½ **cup shredded cooked chicken**	**4 slices very thin white bread**
1½ **teaspoons soy sauce**	**Butter**

Wash bean sprouts thoroughly and pinch off both ends of each. Put into a strainer. Pour the boiling water over them. Rinse with cold water for about 2 minutes. Drain thoroughly. Put into a bowl and chill at least an hour. Add ham, chicken and other ingredients, except bread and butter. Mix well. Spread two slices of bread with some of the mixture; top with remaining two slices bread. Heat open "Double Mac" grill 5 minutes. Melt 1 tablespoon butter on it. Place sandwiches on it; brown bottoms to golden, 1½-2 minutes. Butter the top side of the sandwiches; turn and brown the second side.

Yield: 2 servings

Note: If using "Little Mac" cook one at a time.

* Adds delicious flavor. Found in Oriental shops and in gourmet departments.

3 tablespoons chopped onion
3 tablespoons chopped pimiento
1 cup sliced mushrooms
3 tablespoons butter
¼ teaspoon salt

Dash freshly ground pepper
1 teaspoon flour
4 slices white bread
Butter

In a skillet, saute onion, pimiento and mushrooms in melted butter until tender. Add salt, pepper and flour; cook over low heat, stirring constantly, until slightly thickened. Spread on two slices of the bread. Cover with remaining slices. Heat open "Double Mac" grill 5 minutes. Melt 1 tablespoon butter on it. Place sandwiches on grill and cook until undersides are golden, about 2 minutes. Turn, adding more butter if necessary, and cook 1-2 minutes to brown other side.

Yield: 2 servings
Note: If using "Little Mac" cook one at a time.

SWEET TOOTH SANDWICH

¼ cup orange marmalade
½ cup grated raw carrot
2 tablespoons mayonnaise

4 slices cinnamon-raisin bread
Butter

Mix marmalade, carrot and mayonnaise. Spread on two slices of the bread. Cover with remaining slices. Heat open "Double Mac" grill 5 minutes. Melt 1 tablespoon butter on grill; place sandwiches on top. Cook about 2 minutes, or until lightly browned on bottom. Turn, adding more butter if necessary, and cook 1-2 minutes longer to brown.

Yield: 2 servings
Note: If using "Little Mac" cook one at a time.

1 medium-sized ripe avocado
1 tablespoon mayonnaise
1/8 teaspoon salt
Dash freshly ground pepper

1/8 teaspoon garlic powder
2 teaspoons chili powder
4 slices white bread
Butter

Peel avocado and remove pit. Put through a food mill or mash with a fork until there are no lumps. Mix with other ingredients, except bread and butter. Spread half the mixture on each of two slices of bread. Cover with remaining slices. Heat open "Double Mac" grill 5 minutes. Melt 1 tablespoon butter on it. Put sandwiches on grill; cook until golden on bottom, about 1½ minutes. Turn and brown second side to golden, adding more butter if necessary.

Yield: 2 servings

Note: If using "Little Mac" cook one at a time.

½ small avocado
4 slices crisp bacon, crumbled
2 tablespoons chopped
    blanched almonds

2 tablespoons butter
1 teaspoon lemon juice
4 slices cracked wheat bread

Mash avocado. Combine with bacon and nuts. Spread on two of the bread slices. Top with remaining slices. Blend lemon juice with butter. Heat open "Double Mac" grill 5 minutes. Put half of the lemon butter on grill; when melted, add sandwiches. Spread tops with remaining lemon butter. Cook until bottom slices are golden brown. Turn and cook until second sides are golden.

Yield: 2 servings

Note: If using "Little Mac" cook one at a time.

4 slices whole wheat bread   2 tablespoons strawberry jam
4 tablespoons chunky peanut butter   Butter

Spread 2 slices of bread with peanut butter. Top with jam. Cover with two remaining bread slices. Heat open "Double Mac" grill 5 minutes. Melt 1 tablespoon butter on it. Put on sandwiches and cook until bottoms are brown, about 2 minutes. Turn, adding more butter if needed. Cook until second side is brown.

Yield: 2 servings

Note: If using "Little Mac" cook one at a time.

GRILLED BANANA, HAM AND PEANUT BUTTER SANDWICH

4 slices whole wheat bread   1 small banana, sliced
2 slices boiled ham   1 tablespoon vegetable oil
4 tablespoons peanut butter   1 tablespoon butter

Place a slice of ham on two of the slices of bread. Spread with peanut butter. Place banana slices over peanut butter. Top with remaining bread slices. Heat open "Double Mac" grill 5 minutes. Put oil and butter on it; when hot, put on the sandwiches. Butter tops; cover and cook until golden, about 2 minutes. Turn, butter tops and brown second side.

Yield: 2 servings

Note: If using "Little Mac" cook one at a time.

2 slices rye bread
3 tablespoons peanut butter
2 dried figs

1 teaspoon brown sugar
Butter

Spread one slice of the bread with peanut butter. Cut figs into small pieces; sprinkle over peanut butter. Sprinkle lightly with brown sugar. Cover with second slice of bread. Heat "Mac" fast cooker 5 minutes. Put on sandwich, butter top; cover and cook until lightly browned, about 2 minutes. Turn, butter top, cover and brown other side.

Yield: 1 serving

Note: Waldorf salad goes well with this.

1 3-ounce package cream cheese
Dash salt
¼ cup finely chopped pecans
1 tablespoon syrup from
     ginger bottle

1 teaspoon vinegar
¼ cup finely chopped preserved ginger
4 slices very thin white bread
Butter

Mix all ingredients except bread and butter. Spread on two bread slices. Top with remaining slices. Heat open "Double Mac" grill 5 minutes. Put on butter; when melted, add sandwiches. Cook until golden on bottom, about 2 minutes. Turn, adding more butter if necessary, and brown second side.

Yield: 2 servings

Note: If using "Little Mac" cook one at a time.

Canapes

It's fun to turn a dab of this and that into a mini-meal at the cocktail hour. Guests particularly appreciate something hot to nibble on while they sip iced drinks. It's not hard for the short-order canape cook to whip up some goodies to get things going. You'll find some wonderful ways in the recipes that follow.

In Spain these are served as a main course in larger quantity. They are stripped of shells by the diner and then dipped into sauce. It's an interesting concept for appetizers too.

1 pound shrimp in the shell   **4 tablespoons olive oil**
3 tablespoons coarse salt   **Sauce [see below]**
    [or sea salt]

Place shrimp in a bowl, add salt and toss so that each shrimp is coated with some of it. Heat open "Mac" grill, add oil and, when hot, add some shrimp, using a small wooden spatula to keep them from sticking. As soon as shrimp begin to turn pink, 1 minute or less, sprinkle them with a little olive oil and continue cooking until shrimp are dark pink, about 2 minutes more. Remove shrimp to serving plate. Repeat until all are done.
Yield: 6 servings as appetizers

SAUCE FOR GAMBAS FRESCAS

4 tablespoons minced parsley   **6 tablespoons olive oil**
1 clove garlic, mashed

Mix together and serve with the shrimp as a dip.
Yield: About ½ cup

12 skinless and boneless sardines
½ teaspoon Worcestershire sauce
1 teaspoon chili sauce
1 tablespoon onion, minced fine
1 tablespoon chopped stuffed
   green olives
½ teaspoon salt

Dash paprika
1 tablespoon mayonnaise
12 slices very thin white bread,
   crusts removed
1 tablespoon peanut oil
1 tablespoon butter

Mash sardines and mix with Worcestershire sauce, chili sauce, onion, chopped olives, salt, paprika and mayonnaise. Spread mixture on six of the bread slices. Cover with remaining slices. Cut into quarters. Heat open "Mac" grill 5 minutes. Add oil and butter; when butter melts, add some canapes without crowding them. Cook until golden on bottom, about 2 minutes. Turn and brown second side, adding more butter and oil if needed. Remove, again adding oil and butter if needed, and cook remaining canapes.

Yield: 2 dozen

FRIED CHEESE PUFFS

2 egg whites, beaten stiff
½ cup grated Parmesan cheese
1 tablespoon flour
1/8 teaspoon salt

Dash cayenne
½ teaspoon sweet paprika
Italian seasoned breadcrumbs
½ cup peanut oil

Fold into the stiffly beaten egg whites all the remaining ingredients except breadcrumbs and oil. Chill mixture at least 1 hour. Form into 1" balls and roll in seasoned crumbs. Heat open "Double Mac" grill 5 minutes. Add oil; when hot, add some cheese balls and fry until golden on all sides, about 2-3 minutes. Repeat. Serve at once.

Yield: 20-25 puffs

Note: If using "Little Mac" use less oil and cook in smaller amounts. May be deep fried in "Fry All".

1 tablespoon butter

1 tablespoon minced onion

1 tablespoon minced sweet
    red pepper

1¼ tablespoons flour

¼ cup milk

¼ teaspoon salt

1 teaspoon Dijon mustard

Dash Tabasco

½ cup flaked and picked-over
    crab meat

¼ cup flour

1 egg, beaten

½ cup cornflake crumbs

1 tablespoon vegetable oil

1 tablespoon butter

Melt 1 tablespoon butter in a skillet; cook onion and sweet red pepper until soft but not brown. Add 1¼ tablespoons flour and cook a minute, then stir in milk. Cook, stirring constantly, until mixture boils and becomes very thick. Add salt, mustard and Tabasco. Stir in crab meat. Chill thoroughly. Shape into twelve 1" balls. Dredge balls in flour, dip into beaten egg and roll in crumbs. Heat open "Double Mac" grill 5 minutes. Add oil and butter; when butter melts, add crab balls. Cook, turning over frequently with a wooden spatula until golden on all sides. Drain on paper toweling. Serve warm with cocktails.

Yield: About 1 dozen

Note: If using "Little Mac," use less oil and cook in smaller amounts. May be deep fried in "Fry All".

12 anchovy fillets
2 tablespoons lemon juice
1 teaspoon finely chopped shallot
1 teaspoon finely chopped parsley
½ cup flour

¼ teaspoon salt
1 egg, beaten
1 tablespoon melted butter
½ cup flat beer
Peanut oil

Drain anchovies and place on a plate, none overlapping. Mix lemon juice, shallot and parsley; sprinkle over anchovies. Cover plate with plastic wrap and marinate for 1 hour. Sift together the flour and salt. Add egg and melted butter; mix well. Add beer and stir only until the mixture is smooth. Let stand 1 hour. Drain the fillets from the marinade. Dip each fillet into batter. Heat open "Mac" grill 5 minutes. Add a few tablespoons of peanut oil; when hot, add some of the fritters. Cook to brown on one side, about 2 minutes. Turn, adding more oil if needed, and brown second side. Remove from grill and keep hot. Finish cooking all fritters the same way.
Yield: 12 fritters

CHEESE NUT BALLS

2 teaspoons flour
Dash cayenne
½ teaspoon salt
1 cup grated Swiss cheese

1 egg white, beaten stiff
Pecans, ground fine
Butter

Mix flour, cayenne, salt and grated cheese. Fold in egg white just until well blended. Chill mixture for an hour. Form into small balls and roll in ground pecans. Heat open "Mac" grill 5 minutes. Butter generously and put in as many of the balls as can be accommodated without crowding. Cook, rolling over frequently, until browned to golden on all sides. Remove and keep warm. Cook remaining balls in the same way. Serve hot with cocktail picks.
Yield: About 15

1 9-ounce package frozen crab
   miniatures

2 tablespoons peanut oil
Special Sauce [see below]

Heat open "Double Mac" grill 5 minutes. Add oil; when hot, add frozen crab miniatures. Cook until golden brown on all sides, turning frequently with tongs, about 3 minutes. Serve with Special Sauce.
Yield: 4-6 servings as a canape
Note: If using "Little Mac," cook half package at a time.

SPECIAL SAUCE

3 tablespoons mayonnaise
1 tablespoon chili sauce
1 teaspoon chili powder

2 teaspoons curry powder
Dash garlic powder

Mix all ingredients thoroughly, until mayonnaise is smooth. This sauce can be used with any seafood canape or for dunking raw vegetables.
Yield: About ¼ cup sauce

BACON SURPRISE

6 strips bacon
1 egg
Few drops Tabasco
Few drops Worcestershire sauce

¼ cup very fine breadcrumbs
¼ teaspoon salt
Dash freshly ground pepper
Peanut oil

Cut each slice of bacon into six approximately even pieces. Beat egg with Tabasco and Worcestershire sauce. Combine breadcrumbs, salt and pepper. Dip bacon into seasoned egg, then into seasoned breadcrumbs. When ready to serve, heat open "Mac" grill and fry bacon squares until crisp and brown, 2-3 minutes on each side.
Yield: 3 dozen

These canapes are Puerto Rican in origin and make a good accompaniment to any drink. These may also be deep fried in a "Fry All".

¾ **cup cornmeal**
¼ **teaspoon salt**
½ **to ¾ cup water**

⅓ **cup grated Parmesan cheese**
Peanut oil

Mix cornmeal and salt in a saucepan. Add water gradually, stirring to make a thick mush. Cook for a few minutes, stirring constantly. Add cheese and mix well. Shape into cylinders about ¾" wide and 3" long. Heat open "Double Mac" grill 5 minutes. Add ¼ cup peanut oil. When hot, add Surullitos (not too many at a time or they will be hard to turn) and cook, turning frequently with a small pancake turner, to brown all sides golden. This will take 4-5 minutes. Drain on paper toweling. Cook remainder of mixture until it is used up, adding oil if needed. Serve at once with Ajelimojili Sauce (see below).
Yield: About 14
Note: If using "Little Mac" use less oil and cook in smaller amounts.

AJELIMOJILI SAUCE

2 chili peppers
1 pimiento, well drained
½ teaspoon salt
4 black peppercorns

1 clove garlic
¼ cup lemon juice
¼ cup olive oil

Put peppers, pimiento, salt, peppercorns, garlic and lemon juice into an electric blender. Whirl to grind. Add oil and let stand to meld flavors. Strain and serve as a dip for Surullitos.
Yield: ⅔ cup

2 egg yolks
1 egg white
1 teaspoon finely chopped chives
1 teaspoon finely chopped parlsey
1 teaspoon grated onion
1 teaspoon finely chopped
    green pepper
½ teaspoon salt

Dash freshly ground pepper
Dash nutmeg
1 cup cold potatoes, mashed smooth
1 cup sieved cottage cheese
1 cup very fine breadcrumbs
1 egg
2 tablespoons milk
Peanut oil

Beat egg yolks and white with chives, parsley, onion, salt, pepper and nutmeg. Add mashed potatoes and beat well. Beat in cottage cheese. Form into bite-sized balls. Roll in breadcrumbs. Beat egg and milk together; dip balls in this mixture and then again in breadcrumbs. Chill well. When ready to serve, heat open "Double Mac" grill 5 minutes. Pour in about ¼ cup peanut oil; when hot, add a few of the balls and cook, rolling over frequently, until brown on all sides. Remove with slotted spoon and drain on paper toweling. Keep warm. Continue the same process until all balls are done, adding more oil if necessary.

Yield: About 2 dozen

Note: If using "Little Mac," use less oil and cook fewer each time. May be deep fried in "Fry All".

⅓ **pound chopped chuck**

⅓ **cup prepared poultry stuffing**

1 tablespoon minced onion

1 egg

1/8 teaspoon salt

1 tablespoon peanut oil

Dash freshly ground pepper

1 tablespoon butter

Mix thoroughly all ingredients except oil and butter. Form into bite-sized balls. Heat open "Double Mac" grill 5 minutes. Add oil and butter; when butter melts, add meat balls and brown on all sides, rolling them over frequently to brown.

Yield: 15-20 balls

Note: If using "Little Mac" cook less at a time. Serve with the following sauce for dunking: Mix 1 cup chili sauce with ½ cup grape jelly; heat thoroughly.

1 cup ground, cooked corned beef

Dash freshly ground pepper

2 teaspoons horseradish

2 eggs

2 tablespoons minced onion

1 tablespoon water

2 teaspoons minced parsley

½ **cup cornflake crumbs**

½ **teaspoon salt**

2 tablespoons peanut oil

Dash cayenne pepper

Grind corned beef fine. Mix with seasonings. Beat 1 egg; add. Form into 1" balls. Beat remaining egg in water. Roll balls in egg mixture and then in cornflake crumbs. Heat open "Double Mac" grill 5 minutes. Add oil; when hot, put on corned beef balls and cook, turning frequently, until browned on all sides, 3-4 minutes.

Yield: About 16 balls

Note: If using "Little Mac" cook half at a time.

For superb flavor, buy the smokiest-flavored cocktail sausages you can find. Serve with Dijon mustard, Mustard Sauce (page 73) or Creamy Horseradish Sauce, below.

24 smoke-flavored cocktail sausages

Heat open "Mac" grill 5 minutes. Place some of the sausages on ungreased grill. Cook, turning constantly, until brown on all sides, about 2 minutes. Serve hot with Creamy Horseradish Sauce.
Yield: 2 dozen

CREAMY HORSERADISH SAUCE

½ **cup heavy cream**   **1/8 teaspoon salt**
2 tablespoons lemon juice   **Dash freshly ground pepper**
3 tablespoons grated horseradish,
    well drained

Whip cream until stiff. Fold in lemon juice and horseradish. Season with salt and pepper.
Yield: About 1 cup

1 cup minced cooked chicken	1 egg
1 teaspoon chili powder	1 tablespoon cream
1½ teaspoons minced onion	Butter
¼ teaspoon dry mustard	

Mix all ingredients, except butter, well, and form into thin flat cakes about the size of a half dollar. Heat open "Double Mac" grill 5 minutes. Melt 2 tablespoons butter on it and fry some of the cakes to golden brown, about 1 minute on each side. Drain on paper toweling. Repeat until all are done.

Yield: About 12 kebabs

Note: If using "Little Mac" cook four at a time. Thinly sliced raw onion is usually served with these chicken kebabs.

SAUTEED MUSHROOM CANAPES

½ pound fresh mushrooms	Dash freshly ground pepper
2 tablespoons butter	½ cup cream
2 tablespoons flour	14 slices very thin white bread
1 teaspoon salt	Butter

Remove stems from mushrooms (reserve for other use); chop caps coarsely. Melt 2 tablespoons butter in a skillet; saute mushrooms about 4 minutes, stirring frequently. Add flour, salt and pepper and stir until smooth. Add cream and cook, stirring constantly, until thickened. Cool slightly. Cut 2" rounds from the bread with a cookie cutter. Spread mushroom mixture lightly on half of the bread rounds and top with remaining rounds. Heat open "Mac" grill 5 minutes. Add 2 tablespoons butter; when melted, add some canapes, without crowding. Cook until brown on the bottom, turn and brown second side to golden, adding more butter if needed. Remove from the grill. Cook remaining canapes in the same way, adding butter as needed.

Yield: 21 canapes

Entrees

Cooking for one or two people is simple with a fast cooker, whether you use the open grill or lock on the cover and cook enclosed. Meat, chicken, fish and even vegetables emerge fresh and hot, ready to eat just minutes after you get started. The "Mac" cookers are a boon for people who do not have time to spend hours in the kitchen. They just let "Mac" do it!

1 slice shell steak, ½" thick   **2 tablespoons butter**
1/8 teaspoon salt   **Fried Parsley [page 90]**
Dash freshly ground pepper

Remove the steak from the refrigerator at least an hour before you plan to cook it. Season with salt and pepper. Heat open "Mac" grill 5 minutes. Melt butter on it. Place the steak on the grill and cook 2 minutes on each side, turning once, for rare. Cook longer if desired.

Yield: 1 serving

Note: Serve with Fried Parsley, potatoes of your choice and sliced tomatoes sprinkled with chopped scallions and French dressing.

SPREADS FOR STEAK

Roquefort spread:
Cream 1 ounce of Roquefort cheese with 2 tablespoons butter.
Tabasco spread:
Cream ¼ teaspoon Tabasco and 1 teaspoon Worcestershire sauce with 2 tablespoons butter.
Mustard spread:
Cream 1 tablespoon Dijon mustard with 2 tablespoons butter.

Spread whichever you choose on hot steak just before serving.

CORNED BEEF HASH

1 7¼-ounce can corned beef hash **1 tablespoon butter**
1 tablespoon peanut oil

Open the can of hash at both ends and gently push the hash out in one piece. Cut into four equal slices. Heat open "Double Mac" grill 5 minutes. Put in oil and butter; when butter melts, put in the hash rounds. Cook until browned on one side, about 2 minutes. Turn and brown other side.
Yield: 2 servings
Note: Serve with catsup or chili sauce. A fruit salad would be a nicely contrasting accompaniment, too. If using "Little Mac" cook two at a time.

GINGERED BEEF

¾ pound boneless sirloin of beef **1 small clove garlic, mashed**
2 tablespoons beef stock **1 tablespoon chopped fresh ginger**
2¼ teaspoons soy sauce **2 scallions**
1 teaspoon dry sherry **1½ teaspoons cornstarch**
½ teaspoon sugar **1½ teaspoons water**
2 tablespoons peanut oil

Cut meat into strips ½" thick and about 3" long. Combine stock, soy sauce, sherry and sugar. Set aside. Heat open "Double Mac" grill 5 minutes. Add oil; when hot, saute garlic and ginger for 1 minute. Cut scallions diagonally into ½" pieces and add them with the meat to the grill. Stir-fry with a wooden spatula to brown the meat, about 4 minutes. Add soy sauce mixture and cook for 2 minutes. Mix cornstarch with water and stir in. Cook about 1 minute longer, stirring to coat meat.
Yield: 2-3 servings
Note: Serve with rice and green salad. If using "Little Mac" cook half at a time.

Entrees 65

1⅓ pounds ground lamb
¼ teaspoon salt
1/8 teaspoon freshly ground pepper
¼ teaspoon dried thyme

1 tablespoon cooking oil
1 tablespoon butter
Barbecue sauce [see below]

Mix lamb with seasonings. Form into four patties, each about an inch thick. Heat open "Double Mac" grill for 5 minutes. When hot, add oil and butter. Cook patties 2-3 minutes on each side, turning once. They will be nicely pink in the middle and brown on the outside. Serve with barbecue sauce.

Yield: 2 servings

Note: If using "Little Mac" cook one at a time.

BARBECUE SAUCE FOR LAMB

2 tablespoons sugar
1 teaspoon prepared mustard
Dash freshly ground pepper
1 teaspoon salt
1 teaspoon chili powder
2 tablespoons red wine vinegar
1 cup water

1 cup catsup
2 tablespoons Worcestershire sauce
Dash Tabasco
1 thick slice lemon
1 medium onion, sliced
1 clove garlic, mashed
¼ cup butter

Mix dry ingredients together in a saucepan. Add vinegar, water and catsup; stir well. Add remaining ingredients. Bring to boil, lower heat and cook, uncovered, at a simmer for 20 minutes, stirring frequently. Remove lemon and onion slices.

Yield: About 2 cups

Note: Sauce will keep well in the refrigerator in a jar with a tight lid.

4 lamb kidneys, sliced thin
2 tablespoons butter
1 ounce cognac, warmed
2 teaspoons minced onion
1½ teaspoons minced parsley
¼ cup canned beef gravy
1 tablespoon Madeira

¼ teaspoon Worcestershire sauce
Dash Tabasco
¼ teaspoon lemon juice
2 tablespoons cream
1/8 teaspoon salt
Dash freshly ground pepper

Heat open "Double Mac" grill 5 minutes. Put in butter; when melted, add kidneys and cook, stirring constantly, until slightly browned—about 1 minute. Pour warmed cognac over and ignite. Remove kidneys with a slotted spoon. Add onion, parsley, gravy, Madeira, Worcestershire sauce, Tabasco, lemon juice and cream. Stir with wooden spatula for a minute. Add salt and pepper. Return kidneys to the sauce for just ½ minute.

Yield: 2 servings

Note: Serve with rice and asparagus tips. If using "Little Mac" cook half at a time.

CALF'S LIVER A LA MAC

2 ½"-thick slices calf's liver
1/8 teaspoon salt
Dash freshly ground pepper

Flour
1 tablespoon vegetable oil
1 tablespoon butter

Season slices with salt and pepper; dredge with flour. Heat open "Double Mac" grill 5 minutes. Put in the oil and butter. When butter melts, add liver slices and cook 2 minutes. Turn and cook 2 minutes longer. The liver will be just faintly pink inside and browned to golden.

Yield: 2 servings

Note: If using "Little Mac" cook one at a time.

This is very good with polenta, which is how they serve it in Venice.

½ **pound calf's liver, cut very thin**	**1/8 teaspoon salt**
1 medium onion	**Dash freshly ground pepper**
1 tablespoon butter	**1½ teaspoons dried sage**
1 tablespoon olive oil	**Dash white wine**

Cut the liver into squares. Peel onion and slice very thin. Heat open "Double Mac" grill 5 minutes. Add butter and olive oil; when butter melts, put in onions and cook until soft but not brown. Add liver, salt, pepper and sage. Cook 3-4 minutes, turning occasionally with a wooden spatula. (Do not over-cook or the liver will be tough.) Add white wine and serve at once.

Yield: 2 servings

Note: If using "Little Mac" cook half at a time.

VEAL SCALLOPINI WITH LEMON

2 pieces veal, cut for scallopini,	**Flour**
each about 5" x 3½"	**2 tablespoons butter**
1/8 teaspoon salt	**2 tablespoons lemon juice**
Dash freshly ground pepper	**2 tablespoons finely minced parsley**

Dry the veal very well with paper toweling. Heat open "Double Mac" grill 5 minutes. Meanwhile, season scallopini with salt and pepper and dredge with flour. Melt butter on grill; add scallopini. Cook 1 minute. Turn and cook 1 minute more. Add lemon juice to browned butter on the grill and swirl to mix. Pour over scallopini, sprinkle with minced parsley and serve at once.

Yield: 2 servings

Note: If using "Little Mac" cook half at a time. Serve with rice and sauteed zucchini, if desired.

This dish is very popular in Switzerland, where it is known as Geschnetzeltes Kalbfleisch. Serve with thin noodles.

2 pieces scallopini of veal
   [about 6" x 3"]
2 tablespoons butter
2 teaspoons finely minced scallions
1 teaspoon flour
Dash sweet paprika

2 tablespoons white wine
3 tablespoons canned beef gravy
¼ cup cream
1 teaspoon minced parsley
1 teaspoon minced chives

Cut the pieces of scallopini into pieces about ½" wide, then cut these across. Pat dry on paper toweling. Heat open "Double Mac" grill 5 minutes. Put in butter; when melted, add veal and stir with a wooden spatula about 2 minutes, or until lightly browned. Remove veal from grill; add scallions and fry about ½ minute. Add flour and paprika and stir carefully to mix. Add wine and gravy; when it bubbles, stir in the cream. Return meat to the sauce and turn over fast for about ½ minute, until hot. Serve sprinkled with parsley and chives.

Yield: 2 servings
Note: If using "Little Mac" cook half at a time.

VEAL ALL' UCCELLETTO

2 pieces veal, cut for scallopini
Flour
2 tablespoons olive oil

1 small clove garlic, peeled
1 bay leaf
¼ cup white wine

Dry the veal thoroughly on paper toweling. Dredge lightly with flour. Heat open "Double Mac" grill 5 minutes. Add olive oil, garlic and bay leaf for about 1 minute. Add veal. Cook until golden on bottom, about 1 minute. Turn and brown second side 1 minute. Add wine and, as soon as it foams up, remove garlic and bay leaf. Serve at once with wine gravy poured over.

Yield: 2 servings
Note: If using "Little Mac" cook half at a time.

2 pieces veal, cut for scallopini,
  each about 5" x 3½"
1/8 teaspoon salt
Dash freshly ground pepper

Flour
2 tablespoons butter
3 tablespoons Marsala wine

Dry the veal very well with paper toweling so it will brown nicely. Heat open "Double Mac" grill 5 minutes. Meanwhile, season scallopini with salt and pepper; dredge with flour. Melt butter on grill and add scallopini. Cook 1 minute. Turn and cook 1 minute longer. Add wine and let it foam up. Pour wine gravy over scallopini on serving plates.

Yield: 2 servings

Note: If using "Little Mac" cook half at a time.

2 tablespoons butter
3 tablespoons flour
½ cup milk
1/8 teaspoon salt
Dash freshly ground pepper
2 egg yolks

1 cup diced cooked chicken
4 tablespoons sauteed minced
  mushrooms
Prepared poultry stuffing
Butter

Melt the 2 tablespoons butter and stir in flour smoothly. Gradually add milk, stirring constantly until thickened. Add salt, pepper and egg yolks. Add chicken and mushrooms; stir to blend well. Refrigerate until ready to use. Form into two cakes. Heat open "Double Mac" grill 5 minutes. Butter it lightly. Meanwhile, coat the fritters with prepared poultry stuffing. Place fritters on the grill and cook until browned, 1-2 minutes. Turn and brown the other side, about 1 minute. Serve at once, with mushroom sauce (page 90), if desired.

Yield: 2 servings

Note: If using "Little Mac" cook one at a time.

Rice in the style of Milan, browned in butter while raw, then cooked in chicken broth, is delicious with this chicken, and buttered peas provide a nice color contrast.

1 chicken breast, boned, skinned and cut in half	**1 egg, beaten**
Dash salt	**¼ cup soft white breadcrumbs**
Dash freshly ground pepper	**¼ cup grated Parmesan cheese**
Flour	**1 tablespoon butter**

Season chicken with salt and freshly ground pepper. Sprinkle lightly with flour. Dip into beaten egg. Mix breadcrumbs and cheese; coat chicken with the mixture. Heat open "Double Mac" grill 5 minutes. Melt butter on it. Place chicken on grill; cook 3 minutes to brown lightly. Turn and cook 2-3 minutes on second side to brown to your taste. Serve with browned butter to pour over, if desired.

Yield: 2 servings

Note: If using "Little Mac" cook one at a time.

CAPERY CHICKEN BREAST

1 chicken breast, boned, skinned and cut in half	**1/8 teaspoon thyme**
Flour	**1/8 teaspoon oregano**
1/8 teaspoon onion powder	**1 tablespoon butter**
Dash freshly ground pepper	**1 tablespoon olive oil**
1/8 teaspoon garlic powder	**1 tablespoon capers and**
1/8 teaspoon salt	** ½ teaspoon juice**
	½ cup heavy cream

Dredge chicken with flour mixed with seasonings. Heat open "Double Mac" grill 5 minutes. Add butter and olive oil; when butter melts, add chicken. Cook for about 3 minutes on each side. When chicken is golden brown, add capers. Then pour in cream and let it bubble for 1 minute.

Yield: 2 servings

Note: If using "Little Mac" cook one at a time.

¼ **pound chicken livers**
½ **avocado, peeled and sliced**
1/8 teaspoon salt
Dash freshly ground pepper
Flour

1 tablespoon vegetable oil
1 tablespoon butter
1 teaspoon lemon juice
1 teaspoon minced parsley

Season livers and avocado slices with salt and pepper to taste. Dredge lightly with flour. Heat open "Mac" grill 5 minutes. Add oil and butter; heat until butter melts. Add chicken livers at one side of the grill and avocado slices at the other. Cook about 3 minutes, turning often with a small wooden spatula, or until livers and avocado are nicely browned. The livers will be slightly pink inside and the avocado slices tender. Place on a serving plate and pour pan juices over. Sprinkle livers with a few drops of lemon juice and the parsley.

Yield: 1 serving

Note: If you wish to make this dish for two, double the quantity and cook the livers first; remove them and keep them warm while cooking the avocado slices. If using "Little Mac" cook this way too.

SUPREMES OF CHICKEN, BUTTERMILK FLAVOR

1 chicken breast, boned, skinned
    and cut in half
Dash salt
Dash freshly ground pepper

½ **cup buttermilk**
½ **cup cornflake crumbs**
Butter

Flatten the chicken with the flat of a cleaver. Season with salt and pepper. Dip into the buttermilk, then into cornflake crumbs. Heat open "Double Mac" grill 5 minutes. Melt butter on it. Add chicken and cook until golden brown on one side, about 3 minutes. Turn; brown second side, 2-3 minutes, adding more butter if needed.

Yield: 2 servings

Note: If using "Little Mac" cook one at a time.

1 cup ground cooked ham
1 egg
¼ cup dry breadcrumbs
½ teaspoon Worcestershire sauce

1 tablespoon minced parsley
1 tablespoon minced onion
Milk
2 tablespoons butter

Mix all ingredients except milk and butter. Add enough milk to make mixture of a consistency you can shape. Shape into two patties. Heat open "Double Mac" grill 5 minutes. Add butter; when melted, place patties on grill and cook 3 minutes to brown. Turn and cook another 2-3 minutes until browned to your taste. Serve with Mustard Sauce (see below).

Yield: 2 servings

Note: If using "Little Mac" cook one at a time.

MUSTARD SAUCE

2 tablespoons butter
2 tablespoons flour
1 cup half-and-half cream

1 tablespoon Dijon mustard
1/8 teaspoon salt
Dash freshly ground pepper

Melt butter and stir in flour until smooth. Add cream and cook, stirring constantly, until thickened. Beat in mustard thoroughly. Season with salt and pepper.

Yield: 1 cup

Cooking for one? Buy a ham steak and cook one-third of it. Wrap the rest in heavy duty foil and freeze for a few weeks, or refrigerate for use within several days.

⅓ of the average ham steak,
    ½" thick

⅓ of an 8½-ounce can crushed pine-
    apple in heavy syrup

Heat the open "Mac" grill 5 minutes. Place steak on it without any added fat and cook, turning once, until browned on each side, 3-4 minutes. Remove ham steak and keep warm. Pour pineapple on grill and allow to cook just long enough to brown a little, stirring carefully with a wooden spatula. Spoon pineapple over ham and serve.

Yield: 1 serving

Note: If cooking for 3, all will fit on "Double Mac"; if using "Little Mac" cook one portion at a time.

SCOTCH EGGS

1 cup ground cooked ham
1 raw egg
¼ teaspoon dried leaf thyme
Dash Tabasco

½ teaspoon prepared mustard
2 hard-cooked eggs
Fine dry breadcrumbs
Peanut oil

Mix ham, raw egg, thyme, Tabasco and mustard well. Shell the hard-cooked eggs and wrap in ham mixture. Roll in breadcrumbs. Heat open "Mac" grill 5 minutes. Heat several tablespoons of peanut oil on the grill. Add the coated eggs. Cook, turning to brown on all sides, 3-4 minutes. Cut in half; serve yolk side up on croutons fried in butter, if desired.

Yield: 2 servings

Note: Brussels sprouts and potato pancakes are good with this dish.

Here are a few suggestions for toppings which greatly enhance the pleasure of eating a good hamburger.

Guacamole Topping

Mash a large ripe avocado (about ¾ cup). Stir in 1½ teaspoons lemon juice, 1½ teaspoons grated onion, ¼ teaspoon salt and 6 drops Tabasco. Spoon onto 3 hamburgers and top with slices of peeled ripe tomato.

Blue Cheese-Sour Cream Topping

Mix ⅓ cup crumbled blue cheese with ⅔ cup sour cream and 2 table-spoons thinly sliced scallions. Place a green pepper ring on each of 4 ham-burgers and fill the center with the blue cheese mixture. Top with additional finely sliced scallion, if desired.

Festive Olive Topping

Combine ⅓ cup sliced stuffed green olives, cut in half; ⅓ cup sliced pitted ripe olives, cut in half; 3 tablespoons mayonnaise and 3 tablespoons sour cream. Mix lightly and spoon onto 3 hamburgers.

Mushroom-Pepper Relish Topping

Combine 1 2½-ounce jar sliced mushrooms and 1 tablespoon butter and cook slowly in a saucepan until all liquid evaporates. Stir in 1 tablespoon sliced scallion and ½ cup sweet pepper relish. Mix well and spoon onto 3 ham-burgers just before serving.

Creamy Mustard Topping

Combine ¼ cup prepared mustard, ½ cup mayonnaise and 1 tablespoon very thinly diced onion. Mix well. For 3 or 4 cooked hamburgers.

½ **pound chopped beef**   1/8 **teaspoon pepper**
¼ **teaspoon salt**

Combine chopped beef, salt and pepper. Form into two hamburgers. Place round side in bottom and heat "Double Mac" for 5 minutes. Place hamburgers in circles. Close and cook hamburgers 1 minute on each side for rare, 2 minutes for medium and 3 minutes for well done.

Yield: 2 servings

Note: If using "Little Mac" cook one at a time. If desired, mix meat with up to 2 tablespoons of filling, such as catsup or barbecue sauce, relish, chopped onion, green pepper, mushroom pieces, crumbled bacon, dried onion soup, steak sauce, spices, etc.

CHEESE-STUFFED HAMBURGER IN PIZZA SAUCE

⅔ **pound ground chuck**   **2 1" cubes Mozzarella cheese**
⅓ **cup milk**   **Flour**
Dash garlic powder   **1 tablespoon peanut oil**
1/8 **teaspoon salt**   **1 tablespoon butter**
Dash freshly ground pepper   ½ **cup Pizza Sauce [page 103]**
1 tablespoon minced onion

Mix beef with milk, garlic powder, salt, pepper and onion. Shape mixture into two balls with a cube of cheese in the center of each. Be sure that the cheese is well covered with meat. Dredge balls lightly with flour. Heat open "Double Mac" grill 5 minutes. Add oil and butter. When butter is melted, add hamburgers and cook until browned on bottom, about 2 minutes. Turn and brown second side, adding more butter if needed. Meanwhile, heat Pizza Sauce; serve half of it over each hamburger.

Yield: 2 servings

Note: If using "Little Mac" cook one at a time.

⅓ **pound chopped chuck**
1/8 teaspoon salt
Dash freshly ground pepper

1½ **teaspoons butter**
1½ **teaspoons vegetable oil**
1 teaspoon Worcestershire sauce

Mix beef with salt and pepper and form into a patty, thin if you like it well done, thick if you like it rare. Heat open "Mac" grill 5 minutes. Put in butter and oil and, when butter is melted, add the patty and saute until browned on the bottom, about 2 minutes. Turn and brown the other side. Remove patty and add Worcestershire sauce to the pan drippings. Heat about ½ minute and pour over the hamburger.

Yield: 1 serving

Norwegian hamburgers are called Kjottkaker m/stuet Gronnsaker, but their flavor is not as complicated as their name—just delicious, that's all!

½ **pound ground chuck**
¼ **pound ground lean pork**
½ **teaspoon flour**
½ **teaspoon potato flour**
1/8 teaspoon salt

Dash freshly ground pepper
Dash freshly grated nutmeg
1 tablespoon milk
1 tablespoon water

Mix all ingredients, using just enough milk and water to make them hold together. Form into two cakes. Place round side in bottom of "Double Mac" and heat 5 minutes. Add hamburgers and cook to your taste. Turn and cook other side.

Yield: 2 servings

Note: Serve, if desired, with hot canned beef gravy poured over them and accompanied by mixed cooked vegetables in cream sauce. If using "Little Mac" cook one at time.

⅔ **pound ground chuck**
¼ **cup minced onion**
1 egg
¼ **teaspoon grated lemon peel**

1 tablespoon lemon juice
1 teaspoon salt
Dash freshly ground pepper
½ **teaspoon finely chopped fresh mint**

Mix all ingredients together thoroughly. Shape into two patties. Place round side in bottom of "Double Mac" and heat 5 minutes. Put in burgers and cook to your taste. Turn and cook second side.

Yield: 2 servings

Note: If using "Little Mac" cook one at a time.

½ **pound ground beef**
½ **teaspoon salt**
Dash freshly ground pepper
¼ **cup Italian-flavored breadcrumbs**

1 tablespoon instant minced onion
1 tablespoon cooking oil
2 hamburger buns, split, toasted
   and buttered

Combine beef, salt and pepper. Shape into 4 thin patties. Mix melted butter with breadcrumbs and onion. Divide this onto two of the patties. Top with remaining two patties, pressing edges together firmly. Heat open "Double Mac" grill 5 minutes. Add oil. Cook patties until bottoms are brown, about 3 minutes. Turn and brown second side, about 2 minutes. Place patties in buttered buns.

Yield: 2 servings

Note: If using "Little Mac" cook one at a time. Can be cooked closed (omit oil) in round form.

Kofta is an East Indian way of preparing croquettes. The surprise egg centers make an interesting contrast to the spiced meat.

2 hard-cooked eggs
⅔ pound ground chuck
½ teaspoon ground cardamon
1 teaspoon minced fresh mint
½ teaspoon salt

Dash freshly ground pepper
½ teaspoon ground coriander
2 tablespoons butter
Sauce [see below]

Cut the eggs in half lengthwise. Mix the meat with cardamon, mint, salt, pepper and coriander. Wrap each egg half with meat so no egg shows. Heat open "Double Mac" grill 5 minutes. Melt butter on it. Put in Koftas and brown about 4 minutes on each side. Remove from the "Mac" and keep hot. Make the sauce while the Kofta are cooking.

Yield: 2 servings

Note: If using "Little Mac" cook two at a time.

SAUCE FOR KOFTA

1 tablespoon butter
1 small onion, sliced thin
4 dried red chilis, ground
1 teaspoon turmeric

1 small clove garlic, mashed
½ inch slice of fresh ginger, shredded
½ cup plain yogurt
¼ cup chicken stock

Melt the butter in a skillet. Fry onion, chilis, turmeric, garlic and ginger about 5 minutes. Add yoghurt and chicken stock; heat through. Pour over Kofta.

Yield: 1 cup

2/3 **pound ground chuck**
1/4 **cup mashed banana**
1/4 **cup chopped pecans**
Dash freshly ground nutmeg

Prepared poultry stuffing
1 tablespoon butter
1 tablespoon vegetable oil

Mix meat, banana, pecans and nutmeg. Shape into two thick patties and pat prepared poultry stuffing on all sides. Heat open "Double Mac" grill 5 minutes. Place butter and oil on it; when butter melts, put on the patties and fry until brown on the bottom, about 2 minutes. Turn and fry on the other side until brown.

Yield: 2 servings
Note: If using "Little Mac" cook one at a time.

BLUE CHEESE HAMBURGER

1/3 **pound ground chuck**
1/4 **cup crumbled blue cheese**
1 tablespoon butter
1/2 **teaspoon Worcestershire sauce**

1/4 **teaspoon dry mustard**
1/4 **teaspoon minced onion**
Oil

Shape beef into 4 large thin patties. Mash cheese with a fork. Add butter and mash together until creamy. Add Worcestershire sauce, mustard and onion and mix well. Spread cheese mixture in the center of two of the patties. Top with remaining patties and squeeze the edges together firmly. Heat open "Double Mac" grill 5 minutes. Oil it lightly. Add hamburgers and cook on one side until browned, about 1½ minutes. Turn and cook to brown second side.

Yield: 2 servings
Note: Serve with a salad of grapefruit and endive with French dressing, and hot rolls of your choice. If using "Little Mac" cook one at a time. Can be cooked closed (omit oil) in round form.

⅔ **pound ground chuck**
¾ **cup grated sharp Cheddar**
1 teaspoon minced onion
¼ **teaspoon dry mustard**

1 teaspoon Worcestershire sauce
2 tablespoons butter
3 tablespoons chili sauce

Combine all ingredients except butter and chili sauce and mix thoroughly. Shape into two thick patties. Heat open "Double Mac" grill 5 minutes and add butter. When melted, put in the cheeseburgers and cook 1½-2 minutes to brown bottoms. Turn and brown second sides. Remove cheeseburgers to hot serving plates. Add chili sauce to drippings on the grill. Stir to blend, and pour over cheeseburgers.
Yield: 2 servings
Note: A mixed green salad and corn muffins would make this into a good meal. If using "Little Mac" cook one at a time.

MEAT CAKES

In Norway, whence they come, these are known as Oksekarbonade. They are delicious served with creamed chopped cabbage.

⅔ **pound chopped sirloin**
1 egg
Dash freshly ground pepper
½ **teaspoon salt**

Milk
1 tablespoon butter
Canned beef gravy

Mix meat with egg, pepper, salt and enough milk to make the right consistency to form four flat cakes. Heat open "Double Mac" grill 5 minutes. Add about a tablespoonful of butter; when it melts, put the meat cakes on. Brown on one side about 1 minute. Turn and brown the other side another minute. Serve with heated canned beef gravy.
Yield: 2 servings
Note: If using "Little Mac" shape into long oval cakes and cook two at a time.

Serve with applesauce or with pineapple slices fried along with the meat. Mashed potatoes and red cabbage cooked in sweet-and-sour fashion are good accompaniments.

⅓ **pound ground chuck**
⅓ **pound sausage meat**
2 tablespoons cornflake crumbs

3 tablespoons milk
1 tablespoon chili sauce
Dash salt

Combine thoroughly all ingredients except oil. Shape into two patties. Place round side in bottom and heat "Double Mac" 5 minutes. Add hamburgers; cover and cook 2-3 minutes. Turn and brown other side.
Yield: 2 servings
Note: If using "Little Mac" cook one at a time.

CORN DOGS

⅓ **cup cornmeal**
2½ **tablespoons flour**
½ **teaspoon salt**
1 egg, beaten

1 tablespoon melted butter
¼ **cup milk**
4 frankfurters
Peanut oil

Heat open "Double Mac" grill 5 minutes. Combine cornmeal, flour and salt. Add egg, melted butter and milk. Blend well. Coat each frankfurter with flour and spear it with a fork. Dip into the cornmeal mixture, coating all sides. Pour about ¼ cup peanut oil on grill and allow it to heat for ½ minute. Add frankfurters, two at a time, and cook, turning occasionally, until golden brown on all sides, about 4 minutes. Keep warm and cook the other two frankfurters in the same way.
Yield: 2 servings
Note: May be deep fried in "Fry All"—cut frankfurters in half before coating. If using "Little Mac" use less oil and grill one at a time.

1 7¾-ounce can salmon
4½ teaspoons butter
2 tablespoons chopped onion
1 tablespoon chopped green pepper
¾ cup cold mashed potatoes

1 egg, beaten
1 teaspoon salt
½ teaspoon Worcestershire sauce
Fine breadcrumbs
Vegetable oil

Drain salmon and remove the bones. Place in a bowl and break into small pieces with a fork. Melt butter in a skillet. Add onion and green pepper; saute until soft but not brown. Stir into salmon. Mix in mashed potatoes, beaten egg, salt and Worcestershire sauce. Shape into 4 patties. Cover lightly with breadcrumbs. Refrigerate until ready to cook. Heat open "Double Mac" grill 5 minutes. Grease lightly with vegetable oil. Place patties on grill and cook until golden. Turn, adding more oil if needed, and brown second side. Serve with Cheese Sauce (see below), if desired.

Yield: 2 servings

Note: If using "Little Mac" cook half at a time.

CHEESE SAUCE

1 tablespoon butter
1 tablespoon flour
½ teaspoon salt

½ cup milk
½ cup grated Cheddar cheese

Melt butter in a saucepan. Stir in flour and salt until smooth. Remove from heat and blend in cheese.

Yield: 1 cup sauce

½ cup half-and-half cream
1½ teaspoons butter
½ slice white bread, crust
    removed and torn up
½ teaspoon lemon juice
1 egg, separated
1 cup flaked cooked or canned salmon

1 teaspoon salt
Dash paprika
1 egg, beaten
Cornflake crumbs
1 tablespoon vegetable oil
1 tablespoon butter

Put half-and-half, butter, bread and lemon juice into a saucepan; bring to boil. Beat in the egg yolk. Pour mixture over the salmon and mix well. Beat egg white stiff and fold into mixture. Chill for at least 2 hours. Add salt and paprika. Shape into two cutlets. Dip into beaten egg, then into cornflake crumbs. Heat open "Double Mac" grill 5 minutes. Place oil and butter in it; when butter melts, put in cutlets and cook 2 minutes to brown bottoms. Turn and cook 1½-2 minutes longer. If desired, serve with Orange-Grape Sauce (see below).

Yield: 2 servings
Note: If using "Little Mac" cook half at a time.

ORANGE-GRAPE SAUCE

1 tablespoon cornstarch
1 tablespoon sugar
½ cup orange juice
½ cup cold water
2 teaspoons grated orange rind

1 teaspoon lemon juice
1 11-ounce can mandarin orange
    segments, drained
1 cup seeded green grape halves

Combine cornstarch and sugar in a small saucepan. Stir in orange juice and cold water. Cook slowly, stirring constantly, until thickened. Stir in orange rind, lemon juice, orange segments and grapes. Heat well.

Yield: About 2½ cups sauce

1 cup flaked smoked salmon,
    about 6 ounces
¾ cup seasoned mashed potatoes
1 egg, slightly beaten

½ teaspoon grated onion
Dash freshly ground pepper
¼ cup cornflake crumbs
Butter

Combine fish, potatoes, egg, onion and pepper. Beat until smooth. Chill well. Form into 6 balls. Roll in the crumbs. Heat open "Double Mac" grill 5 minutes. Butter generously. Put in balls and cook, turning occasionally, until browned on all sides, 3-4 minutes.

Yield: 2 servings
Note: If using "Little Mac" cook half at a time.

SAUTEED BROOK TROUT

If you're lucky enough to have a fisherman in the family, maybe you'll be lucky enough to get some fresh brook trout every now and then. Here's an easy way to prepare it:

1 brook trout 7" long or less
1/8 teaspoon salt
Dash freshly ground pepper
Cornmeal

1 tablespoon peanut oil
1 tablespoon butter
Lemon wedge
Minced parsley

Clean trout, leaving head and tail on. If too long for open "Double Mac" grill, remove tail. Sprinkle trout with salt and pepper. Roll in cornmeal. Heat grill 5 minutes. Add oil and butter; when butter has melted, put in fish. Cook 3 minutes to brown bottom. Turn and cook second side 2 minutes to brown until golden. Pour pan drippings over fish on plate. Serve with a lemon wedge and sprinkle with minced parsley.

Yield: 1 serving
Note: If using "Little Mac" cut off tail and place fish diagonally on grill.

Perhaps you prefer to use frozen fish cakes to save time. If so, defrost, then follow the cooking instructions below. Serve with Tomato Sauce that follows—handy to have in the refrigerator for other uses too.

½ **pound salt codfish**	**1 egg, beaten**
3 cups hot mashed potatoes	**Butter**
Dash freshly ground pepper	**Tomato Sauce [see below]**

Soak codfish in cold water 2 hours. Drain. Add fresh water and bring to a boil. Simmer 15 minutes. Drain, shred and add to mashed potatoes with the pepper and egg. Beat thoroughly. Form into three cakes. Heat open "Double Mac" grill 5 minutes. Add a little butter and place cakes on grill. Cook 2 minutes to brown bottom side. Turn and cook 1-2 minutes more to brown second side. Serve with Tomato Sauce.

Yield: 3 servings

Note: Unused portion of mixture can be kept in refrigerator for a few days. If using "Little Mac" cook one at a time.

TOMATO SAUCE

3 tablespoons butter	**1 teaspoon salt**
1 stalk celery, finely chopped	**1 tablespoon sugar**
1 medium onion, chopped	**Dash ground pepper, to taste**
1 tablespoon chopped parsley	**1 teaspoon dried basil [or 2**
1 clove garlic, mashed	**teaspoons, chopped fresh]**
1 29-ounce can tomatoes	**1 bay leaf**
1 tablespoon tomato paste	

Melt butter in a saucepan; lightly brown celery, onion, parsley and garlic. Add tomatoes, tomato paste, salt, sugar and pepper. Simmer gently 45 minutes. Add basil and bay leaf; simmer 15 minutes longer. Remove bay leaf.

Yield: About 3 cups

Note: Sauce will keep for several weeks in a well-sealed jar in the refrigerator.

2 frozen fried fish fillets   **1 serving frozen French-fried potatoes**
2 tablespoons peanut oil

Heat open "Double Mac" grill 5 minutes. Add oil; when hot, place frozen fillets at one side and some frozen French-fried potatoes at other side. Cook fillets 2 minutes on each side, until well browned. Keep turning over potatoes with a spatula until they are browned on all sides, about 5 minutes. Serve with Tartare Sauce (page 92) or with catsup or chili sauce if preferred.
Yield: 1 serving
Note: If using "Little Mac" cook half at a time.

The above recipe is an easy way to make fish 'n' chips—a favorite British combination. It's not difficult to make from scratch. Here's how:

⅔ pound pollock fillets,   **¼ teaspoon salt**
     or other fish   **2-3 tablespoons peanut oil**
½ cup prepared pancake mix   **2 servings French fries,**
½ cup milk   **homemade or frozen**

Cut fillets into 4" x ½" pieces. Combine pancake mix, milk and salt. Beat until smooth. Dip fish pieces into batter. Heat open "Double Mac" grill 5 minutes. Add oil; when hot, add fillets. Cook 2 minutes on each side, or until golden brown. Drain on paper toweling. Cook French fries on grill and serve.
Yield: 2 servings
Note: If using "Little Mac" cook half at a time.

1 11-ounce package frozen
fish sticks

2 tablespoons peanut oil

Heat open "Double Mac" grill 5 minutes. Add oil; when hot, add some of the fish sticks. Cook, turning frequently with tongs, until golden brown on all sides, about 4 minutes. Repeat until all are cooked.

Yield: 4 servings

Note: If fewer servings are desired, remove fish sticks needed and put remainder back into freezer at once. Serve with Remoulade Sauce, below. If using "Little Mac" cook half at a time.

REMOULADE SAUCE

1 cup mayonnaise
¼ cup finely chopped sour pickles
1 tablespoon finely chopped capers

1½ teaspoons Dijon mustard
1½ teaspoons finely chopped parsley

Drain pickles and capers thoroughly before chopping. Mix all ingredients well; serve cold with hot fish.

Yield: 1½ cups

FRIED SMELTS

4 smelts
¼ teaspoon salt
1/8 teaspoon freshly ground pepper

Flour
2 tablespoons butter
1 tablespoon lemon juice

Season whole smelts with salt and pepper. Dredge in flour. Heat open "Double Mac" grill 5 minutes. Melt butter in it. Add smelts and cook 2 minutes on one side. Turn and cook 2 minutes on other side. Remove from grill to serving plates. Pour pan juices over. Sprinkle lightly with lemon juice. Serve with Tartare Sauce (page 92) or Sauce Gribiche (page 89).

Yield: 2 servings

Note: If using "Little Mac" cook half at a time.

1 flounder fillet	2 tablespoons butter
Flour	1 teaspoon finely minced parsley
1/8 teaspoon salt	Lemon wedge
Dash freshly ground pepper	Shrimp Sauce [see below], optional

Dredge fillet well with flour; season with salt and pepper. Heat open "Double Mac" grill 5 minutes. Add 2 tablespoons butter; when melted, place fillet in it. Cook 1 to 1½ minutes. Turn and cook 1 minute on the other side. Pour remaining butter from the grill over the fillet and the parsley. Serve with lemon wedge or sauce below.

Yield: 1 serving

Note: If using "Little Mac" cut fillet in half and cook one piece at a time. If sauce is served omit lemon wedge.

SHRIMP SAUCE

¼ pound shrimp	Dash salt
1 tablespoon butter	Juice of ½ lemon

Shell and devein shrimp; cut up coarsely. Heat open "Mac" grill 5 minutes. Add butter. When it melts, add shrimp and cook about 2 minutes, turning frequently, or until pink. Add salt and lemon juice and cook ½ minute longer. Pour over fish and serve at once.

Yield: 1 serving

SAUCE GRIBICHE

1 cup mayonnaise	3 shallots, minced fine
1 tablespoon Dijon mustard	4 small sour pickles, chopped
2 hard-cooked eggs, chopped	1 tablespoon capers, well drained
1½ teaspoons minced parsley	

Mix all ingredients together gently. Sauce keeps well in the refrigerator if tightly covered.

Yield: About 1½ cups

1 flounder fillet

1/8 teaspoon salt

Dash freshly ground pepper

1 egg, well beaten

¼ cup Italian-flavored breadcrumbs

2 tablespoons butter

Lemon wedge

Fried Parsley [see below]

Season fillet. Dip into beaten egg, then into crumbs, coating well. Heat open "Double Mac" grill 5 minutes. Add 2 tablespoons butter. Put in crumbed fillet and cook 1-1½ minutes on one side, or until golden brown. Turn and brown the other side. Serve with lemon wedge and Fried Parsley.

Yield: 1 serving

Note: If using "Little Mac," cut fillet in half and cook one piece at a time.

FRIED PARSLEY

Pull off little bunches of parsley leaves with a bit of the stems attached. Heat open "Double Mac" grill 5 minutes. Pour in ½ cup peanut oil and, when it is hot, toss in a small handful of the parsley and allow it to cook 1-2 minutes. Be sure it does not burn. Remove with slotted spoon and drain on paper toweling. Cook as much as you wish to use, adding more oil if necessary. Serve at once.

Note: If using "Little Mac," use less oil each time.

MUSHROOM SAUCE

¼ pound mushrooms

¾ cup water

2 tablespoons butter

2 tablespoons flour

½ cup half-and-half cream

Dash salt

Dash freshly ground pepper

Stem the mushrooms and, if necessary, peel them. Put stems and peelings into a small saucepan and cover them with water. Simmer until liquid is reduced to about ½ cup; strain and reserve liquid. Chop mushroom caps coarsely. Melt butter and saute chopped mushrooms 5 minutes. Add flour and stir until smooth. Add half-and-half and strained mushroom liquid and stir until thickened. Season to taste.

Yield: About 1 cup

2 butterfish	2 tablespoons toasted sesame seeds
1/8 teaspoon salt	1 tablespoon peanut oil
Dash freshly ground pepper	1 tablespoon butter
Flour	

Salt and pepper the butterfish and dredge lightly with flour. Roll in sesame seed. Heat open "Double Mac" grill 5 minutes. Add oil and butter; when butter is melted, put in fish. Cook 2 minutes on one side. Turn and cook 2 minutes on second side, or until golden.

Yield: 2 servings

Note: If using "Little Mac" cook one at a time. Butterfish are delicious when accompanied by Fried Parsley (page 90).

FRIED OYSTERS

12 oysters	1 tablespoon vegetable oil
1 cup well crumbled poultry stuffing	1 egg, well beaten
1 tablespoon butter	Lemon wedges

Dip oysters into crumbled stuffing, then into beaten egg, then roll again in stuffing. Heat open "Double Mac" grill 5 minutes. Add oil and butter; when butter melts, add oysters. Cook, turning frequently, until golden on all sides, about 2-3 minutes. Serve with lemon wedges.

Yield: 2 servings

Note: This may be deep fried in "Fry All". If using "Little Mac" cook half at a time.

1 10-ounce can minced clams
2 tablespoons butter
2 teaspoons minced onion
2 teaspoons minced green pepper
Dash thyme
2 tablespoons flour

⅓ cup half clam juice, half milk
1/8 teaspoon salt
Dash freshly ground pepper
Italian-flavored breadcrumbs
Butter
Tartare Sauce

Open can of clams and drain, reserving juice. Melt butter in a skillet; saute onion and green pepper until soft but not brown, stirring frequently. Add thyme and flour; stir until smooth. Add clam juice mixture and stir constantly until thickened. Add clams and season. Refrigerate until ready to use. Form into two round cakes and coat with breadcrumbs. Heat open "Double Mac" grill 5 minutes. Butter it lightly. Place fritters on grill and cook until browned on one side, 1-2 minutes. Turn and brown the other side, about 1 minute. Serve at once with Tartare Sauce below.

Yield: 2 servings

Note: If using "Little Mac" cook one at a time.

TARTARE SAUCE

1 cup mayonnaise

¼ cup sweet pickle relish

Combine mayonnaise and relish. Makes 1¼ cups sauce.

These are among the most delicious shellfish available. "Mac's" quick cooking action prevents any toughening of the delicate fibers.

½ **pound bay scallops***   **Dash salt**
Flour   **Dash freshly ground pepper**
1 tablespoon peanut oil   **2 lemon wedges**
1 tablespoon butter

Dry scallops thoroughly with paper toweling. Dredge lightly with flour. Heat open "Double Mac" grill for 5 minutes. Add oil and butter; when butter melts, add scallops. Cook, turning constantly until delicately browned on all sides, about 1 minute. Sprinkle with salt and pepper to taste. Serve at once with pan drippings poured over, if desired, and with a wedge of lemon.
Yield: 2 servings
Note: If using "Little Mac" cook half at a time.
* If you can't get bay scallops, buy sea scallops and cut each into quarters before flouring them. Good, but not as delicate as the bay variety.

FRIED SCALLOPS

¾ **pound sea scallops**   **Cornflake crumbs**
Flour   **1 tablespoon vegetable oil**
1 egg, beaten   **1 tablespoon butter**

Wash scallops and pat dry with paper toweling. Dredge with flour. Dip into egg and then into cornflake crumbs. Heat open "Mac" grill 5 minutes. Add oil and butter; when butter melts, add scallops, a few at a time. Cook until golden brown on all sides, turning frequently. Repeat, using more butter and oil if necessary. Keep warm until all scallops are cooked. Serve with Tartare Sauce (page 92).
Yield: 2 servings

A frittata is the Italian version of an omelet. Unlike the French type, these omelets are cooked through and browned on both sides.

6 medium shrimp	**Dash Tabasco**
2 eggs, room temperature	**1 teaspoon minced chives**
1 tablespoon water	**1 tablespoon grated Parmesan cheese**
½ teaspoon salt	**1˙tablespoon butter**

Plunge shrimp into boiling water and allow water to return to the boil. Cook until shrimp turn pink, 1-2 minutes. Chop coarsely. Beat eggs very lightly with a fork. Beat in water, salt, Tabasco, chives and cheese. Add shrimp. Heat open "Double Mac" grill 5 minutes. Melt butter on one side. Pour in the egg mixture and, using a fork, see that it does not run beyond the center of the grill. (Be careful to use the back of the fork so as not to scratch the grill.) Cook 2 minutes on the first side until delicately browned. Turn and cook 1 minute longer to brown the other side.

Yield: 1 serving

Note: If you wish to make frittata for two, double the recipe and try to keep a separation down the center of the "Double Mac" grill so the omelet will be easier to turn. If using a "Little Mac" grill make one at a time.

CORN FRITTERS

1 egg, separated	**½ teaspoon sugar**
1½ cups raw, frozen or drained	**1 tablespoon melted butter**
canned corn niblets	**½ teaspoon salt**
2 tablespoons milk	**2 tablespoons butter**
1½ teaspoons flour	

Beat egg yolk lightly and add to corn. Add milk, flour, sugar, melted butter and salt. Beat egg white stiff; fold into batter. Heat open "Double Mac" grill 5 minutes. Butter it well. Fry batter by tablespoonsful until brown and crisp on both sides. Drain on paper toweling.

Yield: 20 fritters

Note: If using "Little Mac" cook a few at a time.

1 small onion, finely chopped	1 egg yolk
2 tablespoons finely chopped green pepper	1 teaspoon Worcestershire sauce
	Dash Tabasco
1 pimiento, finely chopped	½ pound crab meat, picked over
3 tablespoons butter	¾ cup dry breadcrumbs
3 tablespoons flour	2 teaspoons chopped parsley
¼ cup clam juice	Breadcrumbs
¼ cup dry white wine	Butter

In a skillet, saute onion, green pepper and pimiento in butter until soft but not brown. Add flour and cook 3 minutes, stirring constantly. Add clam juice and wine. Cook, stirring, until thickened. Add egg yolk, Worcestershire sauce and Tabasco. Mix in crab meat, ¾ cup breadcrumbs and parsley. Chill for several hours. When ready to cook, form into 4 cakes, 3" wide and 1" thick. Roll in breadcrumbs. Heat open "Double Mac" grill 5 minutes. Add butter; when melted, put on two of the crab cakes and cook until golden brown on the bottom, 2-3 minutes. Turn, adding more butter if necessary, and cook second side until golden brown, about 2 minutes. Serve with Tartare Sauce (page 92).

Yield: 2 servings

Note: If using "Little Mac" cook half at a time.

RICE CAKES

1 cup cold cooked rice	Dash freshly ground pepper
1 egg, lightly beaten	1 tablespoon butter
1/8 teaspoon salt	Crisp bacon

Mix rice with egg and seasonings. Form into 2 large or 4 small cakes. Heat open "Double Mac" grill 5 minutes. Add butter; when melted, put in the rice cakes and cook on one side 2 minutes, until golden brown. Turn and cook the second side, about 1½ minutes. Serve with crisp bacon and Tomato Sauce (page 86).

Yield: 2 servings

Note: If using "Little Mac" cook half at a time. A green salad with French dressing and hot rolls makes this a good supper.

4 soft shell crabs
¼ teaspoon salt
1/8 teaspoon freshly ground pepper
Flour

¼ cup butter
¼ cup slivered blanched almonds
Lemon wedges

Have your fish market clean the crabs. The smaller they are the more delicate and delicious in flavor. Season the crabs with salt and pepper and dredge them with flour on one side. Heat the open "Double Mac" grill 5 minutes. Melt the butter and put the crabs onto the grill, floured side down. Saute 1½-2 minutes, never longer, until lightly browned. Salt and pepper the top side, dredge with flour and turn the crabs. Cook 1½ minutes longer, until lightly brown. Remove crabs and keep warm. Put the almonds into the remaining butter and stir gently until they are golden brown, about ½ minute. (A small wooden spatula is good for this, as it is not likely to scratch the "Mac".) Serve with lemon wedges.

Yield: 2 servings
Note: If using "Little Mac" cook one or two at a time, depending on size.

BROCCOLI FRITTATA

2 eggs, room temperature
1 tablespoon water
½ teaspoon salt
Dash Tabasco
½ teaspoon thyme

½ teaspoon oregano
1 tablespoon grated Parmesan cheese
½ cup minced cooked broccoli
1 tablespoon butter

Beat eggs very lightly with a fork. Add water, salt, Tabasco, herbs, cheese and broccoli. Heat open "Double Mac" grill 5 minutes. Melt butter on one side. Pour in the egg mixture and, using the back of a fork, see that it does not run beyond the center of the grill. Cook 2 minutes on the first side, until delicately browned. Turn and cook 1 minute longer to brown the other side.

Yield: 1 serving
Note: If you wish to make this for two, see note at end of Shrimp Frittata.

4 hard-cooked eggs	Dash freshly ground pepper
1 small onion	1 egg, beaten
2 tablespoons butter	Yellow cornmeal
1 tablespoon flour	1 tablespoon cooking oil
¼ cup milk	1 tablespoon butter
1/8 teaspoon salt	

Chop the eggs and onion together as fine as possible. Melt 2 tablespoons butter and stir in flour until smooth. Add milk, stir constantly until thickened. Mix with the eggs and onion and season with salt and pepper. Chill thoroughly until ready to cook. Shape into six oval croquettes. Dip into the egg, then coat thoroughly with cornmeal. Heat open "Double Mac" grill 5 minutes. Add oil and 1 tablespoon butter. When butter melts, add croquettes and brown well on all sides, about 4 minutes altogether. Serve with Cheese Sauce (page 83).

Yield: 2-3 servings

Note: If using "Little Mac" cook two at a time.

1 cup cold mashed potatoes	Butter
Flour	

Shape potatoes into two round cakes. Dredge with flour. Heat open "Mac" grill 5 minutes. Add 1 tablespoon butter; melt. Add potato cakes; brown one side to golden, about 2 minutes. Turn and brown other side, adding more butter if needed.

Yield: 2 servings

Note: If using "Little Mac" cook one at a time.

2 tablespoons butter
2 tablespoons minced onion
2 tablespoons minced green pepper
1 small clove garlic, mashed
5 tablespoons flour
½ cup milk
1 tablespoon tomato paste

1/8 teaspoon salt
Dash freshly ground pepper
2 tablespoons minced parsley
1¼ cups well-drained canned
    kidney beans
Italian-flavored breadcrumbs
2 tablespoons butter

In a skillet, melt 2 tablespoons butter; cook onion, green pepper and garlic until soft but not brown. Add flour and stir to mix well. Add milk and stir constantly until very thick. Be careful not to burn. Add tomato paste, salt and pepper, parsley and kidney beans. Chill in refrigerator at least 2 hours. Form into 2 large fritters and coat well with breadcrumbs. Heat open "Double Mac" grill 5 minutes. Melt 1 tablespoon of butter on grill; add fritters and cook 2 minutes, or until golden brown. Add another tablespoon of butter and turn to brown second side.

Yield: 2 servings

Note: If using "Little Mac" cook half at a time. These large cutlets are a full portion for a vegetarian; if serving meat, make 4 small cutlets instead, to be served to 4.

These fritters were inspired by the vegetarian cuisine of India. Their delicate quality makes them a good selection for an all-vegetable meal or as an accompaniment to meat.

1 10-ounce package frozen mixed vegetables, or 1¼ cups mixed leftover cooked vegetables
1 tablespoon minced onion
2 tablespoons butter
3 tablespoons flour

1 tablespoon curry powder
½ cup milk
1 egg, well beaten
Prepared poultry stuffing
4 tablespoons butter

Cook vegetables according to package directions. Drain well. Add onion. Melt 2 tablespoons butter in a skillet; stir in flour and curry powder until smooth. Add milk and cook, stirring constantly, until thickened. Stir in egg. Add vegetables and mix well. Chill in refrigerator until ready to use. Heat open "Double Mac" grill 5 minutes. Meanwhile, form 4 fritters. Cover them well with poultry stuffing. Melt 2 tablespoons butter on the grill. Put in 2 fritters and cook 2 minutes to brown to golden. Turn, cook 2 minutes longer, or until browned to your taste. Repeat.

Yield: 4 servings
Note: If using "Little Mac" grill cook one at a time.

1 cup narrow flat noodles
2 tablespoons peanut oil
1½ teaspoons slivered fresh ginger

1 scallion, sliced thin, both
   white and green parts
¼ cup chicken stock
Chinese oyster sauce*

Cook the noodles in boiling salted water 8 minutes. Drain. Heat open "Double Mac" grill 5 minutes and add the oil. When it is hot, in about ½ minute, add ginger and scallion and cook, stirring constantly with the back of a fork, 1 minute. Add a little stock and cook until evaporated. Continue, adding more stock and letting it evaporate until the last lot is not quite evaporated. Add the drained noodles at once and toss gently until they are heated through, about ½ minute. The noodles will be shiny from the oil which remains in the pan. Serve with a little individual dish of oyster sauce into which to dunk the noodles. Or, if preferred, pour a small amount of the sauce over the noodles and toss so that all are lightly coated.

Yield: 1 serving
Note: If using "Little Mac" cook half at a time.
* Obtainable in any Chinatown, other Oriental shops or fine gourmet departments.

GRILLED CUCUMBER SLICES

1 large cucumber
½ teaspoon coarse salt
Dash freshly ground pepper
Dash freshly grated nutmeg

1 egg, beaten
Fine cracker crumbs
Peanut oil

Peel cucumber and slice it into a bowl. Sprinkle with salt and allow to stand for 30 minutes. Drain, season with pepper and nutmeg. Heat open "Mac" grill 5 minutes. Add a couple of tablespoons of oil. Meanwhile, dip cucumber slices in egg, then in crumbs, again in egg and lastly in crumbs. When oil is hot, put in half the cucumber slices and cook until golden brown on the bottom, about 2 minutes. Turn and brown second side, adding more oil if needed, about 1 minute. Remove slices and cook remaining pieces in the same way.

Yield: 2 servings
Note: If using "Little Mac" grill, cook smaller amounts each time.

1 small eggplant	1 tablespoon milk
¼ teaspoon salt	½ cup ground pecans
1/8 teaspoon freshly ground pepper	½ cup cornflake crumbs
Flour	1 tablespoon vegetable oil
1 egg	1 tablespoon butter

Cut four ½"-thick slices from the eggplant. (Save remainder for another time.) Season with salt and pepper. Dredge lightly with flour. Mix eggs and milk; dip slices into egg mixture. Combine pecans and cornflake crumbs; roll slices in the mixture to coat well. Heat open "Double Mac" grill for 5 minutes. Add oil and butter; when butter melts, add two slices of eggplant. Cook 4 minutes on first side. Turn and cook 2 minutes on second side. Remove, keep warm, and cook the remaining slices in the same way, adding more butter if needed.

Yield: 2 servings

Note: If using "Little Mac" grill, cook one at a time.

FRIED CHEESE
[*Smazeny Emental*]

This is a dish which is served all over Czechoslovakia and is delicious with a salad, for either lunch or supper.

8 pieces Swiss cheese, ½" thick, 1½" square	Flour
	Very fine breadcrumbs
1 egg	2 tablespoons butter
2 tablespoons milk	

Cut cheese pieces the same thickness or else they will not cook properly in the same length of time. Beat the egg and milk together. Dredge the cheese pieces with flour, dip into the egg mixture, then coat well with breadcrumbs. Heat open "Mac" grill 5 minutes. Melt the butter on it. Place cheese pieces on the grill; cook 1 minute on the first side to golden brown. Turn and cook 1 minute on the second side. Serve at once.

Yield: 2 servings

Note: If using "Little Mac" cook half at a time.

3 small Chinese dried mushrooms
1 tablespoon minced onion
2 tablespoons cooked peas
½ teaspoon salt

1 tablespoon peanut oil
⅓ cup chicken stock
½ teaspoon soy sauce
1 teaspoon cornstarch, mixed with
    1 teaspoon water

Soak the dried mushrooms in warm water for ½ hour. Drain and shred. Heat the peanut oil in a skillet; fry mushrooms and onion about 5 minutes (do not brown). Add peas, salt, chicken stock and soy sauce. When sauce comes to a boil, thicken with cornstarch mixture. Keep warm until eggs are ready.

THE EGGS

⅓ cup diced cooked shrimp
½ teaspoon minced fresh ginger
2 tablespoons bean sprouts, both
    ends snipped off

1 teaspoon white wine
3 eggs
¼ teaspoon salt
2 tablespoons peanut oil

Mix shrimp, ginger, bean sprouts and wine. Beat eggs lightly with salt; add to mixture. Heat open "Double Mac" grill 5 minutes. Add the peanut oil. Pour in egg-shrimp mixture at each side of the grill, leaving an open space down the center. Fry until golden on bottom, about 2 minutes. Turn and fry second side to golden. Pour sauce over Egg Fu Yung and serve at once.

Yield: 2 servings
Note: If using "Little Mac" fry one at a time.

2 smallest size rounds of
    Arabic bread
Olive oil
Pizza Sauce [see below]

8 medium mushrooms, sliced and
    sauteed in butter 3 minutes
½ cup slivered Mozzarella cheese
½ cup grated Parmesan cheese

In order to make the pizza fit into the square plate of the "Little Mac," cut a little off the outside edge of each Arabic bread round (about ¼"). At this point it is easy to pull the halves of the bread apart. (Use one half for each pizza.) Lightly paint both sides of the split bread with olive oil. Spread a thin coating of Pizza Sauce over each piece. Place ¼ of the mushrooms on top of each. (See below for alternate garnishes.) Cover each pizza with about 2 tablespoons of Mozzarella and top with 2 tablespoons of Parmesan. Heat "Little Mac" 5 minutes. Place pizza on the square plate. Place top cover at right angles to the bottom tray to avoid squashing the pizza too much. Cook for 5 minutes. Remove and start the next pizza.

Yield: 4 servings

Note: If using "Double Mac" arrange 2 pizzas side by side on flat surface.

PIZZA SAUCE

1 15½-ounce can Pizza Sauce
1 teaspoon sugar
½ teaspoon oregano

Dash garlic powder
1 teaspoon minced onion

Heat all ingredients together in a saucepan until bubbling. Leftover sauce may be stored in the refrigerator in a jar with a tight-fitting lid.

Yield: 2 cups

ALTERNATE GARNISHES FOR PIZZA

Canned mushrooms instead of fresh; thinly sliced pepperoni; thinly sliced hot Italian sausage; sliced or chopped green pepper; cooked crisp bacon or anchovy fillets. Professionally made pizzas usually are garnished with at least two of these.

Salads

   For good nutrition as well as taste, the best thing to serve with a "Mac" fast cooker luncheon or supper is a fresh salad. Here are a variety of salads —some with simple descriptions, others with whole recipes, and all easy to prepare. Choose ingredients that are not duplicated in the main dish, and vary your menus with some of the piquant dressings at the end of this chapter.

GREEN SALAD: This is the simplest of all and perhaps the most popular as an accompaniment to other food. Boston lettuce, Bibb lettuce, romaine, chicory, endive, Belgian endive, watercress, dandelion greens and spinach are some of the greens which can be used singly or with one, two or three of the others. Greens should be washed and dried well, then stored in the refrigerator to crisp, as soon as they are picked from the garden or brought home from the market. Wrap them in a tea towel for old-fashioned but effective crisping in the refrigerator.

CHILEAN ENSALADAS: Thin slivers of celery and red radish, marinated 5 minutes or longer in lemon juice, olive oil, salt and pepper. Pour at the last minute over thin slices of avocado.

MANDARIN ORANGES AND BIBB LETTUCE: Add French Dressing (page 112) and serve with fish dishes.

SLICED TOMATOES WITH CHOPPED SCALLIONS: Sprinkle French Dressing (page 112) over tops for a colorful combination.

COLESLAW WITH SOUR CREAM DRESSING: Shred cabbage and add dressing on page 112.

MIXED COOKED VEGETABLE SALAD: Use either leftover vegetables or cooked frozen mixed vegetables; mix with mayonnaise and serve on lettuce. Never use beets, as they stain the whole salad to an unattractive color.

WALDORF SALAD: Diced apples, celery and walnuts in mayonnaise. Serve it on a bed of watercress for variety.

HEARTS OF PALM (canned): With grated hard-cooked egg, minced parsley and French Dressing (page 112).

GRAPEFRUIT SECTIONS AND SPANISH ONION: Thinly sliced. French Dressing (see page 112).

WATERCRESS, TOMATO, CHOPPED ANCHOVY FILLETS, GRATED HARD-COOKED EGG: With French Dressing (see page 112).

CHIFFONADE SALAD: Lettuce, watercress and julienne beets. French Dressing (see page 112).

FRESH FRUIT SALAD: Use melon balls; strawberries; raspberries; blackberries; cherries (pitted); bananas, cut up; blueberries; black currants; red currants; peaches; fresh apricots; skinned and seedless grapes; pineapple cubes or any other fruit which appeals. Serve on lettuce with either mayonnaise, French Dressing or Fruit Salad dressing (see page 113).

APPLE AND CABBAGE SALAD: Dice apples and sliver cabbage. Mix with mayonnaise.

AVOCADO AND COTTAGE CHEESE: Make a pile of cottage cheese in the middle of each salad plate. Surround with thin slices of avocado and pour over French Dressing (see page 112) with chives in it.

COLD COOKED ASPARAGUS: French Dressing (see page 112), pimiento strips, grated hard-cooked egg.

NAVEL ORANGE SECTIONS, BIBB LETTUCE, SWEET RED ONION RINGS: French Dressing (see page 112).

COLD COOKED LEEKS: With French Dressing (see page 112).

RAW MUSHROOM SALAD: Diced onion, red radish, celery and minced parsley marinated for 10 minutes in dressing made from olive oil, lemon juice, cracked pepper and coarse salt, then poured over sliced raw mushrooms and tossed. Serve on lettuce leaves.

BERMUDA ONION AND RIPE OLIVES: Thinly sliced onion and olives with pepper dressing (see page 112).

HEARTS OF PALM AND RAW ZUCCHINI: Sliced. French Dressing (see page 112).

MIMOSA SALAD: Bibb and Romaine lettuce, French Dressing (see page 112) and grated hard-cooked egg yolk sprinkled over.

TOMATO AND SPANISH ONION: Slice tomato and onions very thin and layer them, sprinkling each layer with minced parsley. Pour on French Dressing (see page 112) and sprinkle top with chopped chives. Let stand in a cool place 1 hour before serving.

COLD CURRIED RICE

2 tablespoons butter
½ cup long-grain rice
¾ cup chicken broth

1 teaspoon curry powder
1 cup cooked peas
French dressing [optional]

Melt butter in a saucepan and stir rice in it until every grain is coated and golden in color. Add chicken broth and curry powder and boil 14 minutes. Drain, cool and chill. Mix with peas and the French dressing, if desired. Or serve Major Grey's chutney (a type, not a brand) with the rice.
Yield: 2 servings

2 cups torn greens	1½ tablespoons French Dressing
⅓ cup yoghurt	½ teaspoon celery seed

Place greens in a bowl. Mix remaining ingredients and pour over greens. Toss well. See page 112 for French Dressing recipe.

Yield: 2 servings

Note: Dandelion greens and watercress are particularly good this way.

CELERIE REMOULADE

1 celery root	2 teaspoons lemon juice
Boiling water	1/8 teaspoon salt
1 tablespoon boiling water	Dash freshly ground pepper
2 tablespoons Dijon mustard	2 teaspoons minced parsley
2 tablespoons olive oil	

Peel celery root and slice into julienne strips. Cook in boiling water to cover for 4-5 minutes, or until softened but still crisp. Drain well and chill. Beat 1 tablespoon boiling water into the mustard very slowly; beat olive oil in by drops. Sauce should be thick and creamy. Beat in lemon juice gradually. Add salt and pepper. Pour over celery and chill thoroughly. Sprinkle with parsley.

Yield: 2 servings

Note: This may also be served as an appetizer.

2 strips bacon   ½ pound small fresh spinach leaves
2 tablespoons French Dressing [page 112]

Cut slices of bacon into 1" squares; saute until very crisp. Remove from pan. Strain bacon fat into French Dressing. Pour hot dressing and bacon over spinach leaves to wilt them.

Yield: 2 servings

Note: If spinach is not young, be sure to remove veins and stems.

CAESAR SALAD

⅔ cup bread cubes   2 tablespoons crumbled blue cheese
2 tablespoons garlic-flavored   4 teaspoons lemon juice
   olive oil   2 tablespoons olive oil
1 small head Boston lettuce   1/8 teaspoon salt
1 small head romaine   Dash freshly ground pepper
2 tablespoons grated   1 raw egg
   Parmesan cheese

Fry the bread cubes in the garlic-flavored olive oil until golden, stirring frequently. Drain on paper toweling. Wash and crisp greens. Tear into a bowl. Add the cheeses to the greens. Combine lemon juice, 2 tablespoons olive oil, salt and pepper. Pour over greens. Break raw egg over all and toss so that the egg causes cheeses to coat every salad leaf. Add garlic-flavored bread cubes and toss well.

Yield: 2 servings

2 medium-sized potatoes
½ teaspoon salt
¼ teaspoon sugar
½ teaspoon dry mustard
2 tablespoons vinegar

¼ cup olive oil
Paprika
1 clove garlic [for rubbing bowl]
1 small onion, chopped fine
½ green pepper, chopped fine

Cook potatoes in skins. Cool. Heat the vinegar, oil and seasonings to the boiling point. Peel potatoes and cut them into cubes in a bowl which has been rubbed with a cut clove of garlic. Add onion and pepper. Pour hot dressing over. Mix just enough to blend without breaking up the potatoes too much.
Yield: 2 servings

DANISH WILTED CUCUMBERS

1 medium cucumber
¼ cup vinegar
2 tablespoons water
6 tablespoons sugar

½ teaspoon salt
¼ teaspoon freshly ground pepper
2 tablespoons chopped fresh dill

Wash cucumber; do not peel. Slice very thin. Place in a bowl. Mix vinegar, water, sugar, salt and pepper; pour over cucumber and sprinkle with dill. Place a plate directly on top of cucumber and put a weight (such as an unopened 16-ounce can) on top. Store in refrigerator for a day before serving. Pour off excess liquid and serve.
Yield: 2 servings

PEPPER DRESSING

¼ cup olive oil
¼ cup vinegar
1 tablespoon tomato juice
1½ teaspoons finely diced
    sweet red pepper

1½ teaspoons finely diced
    green pepper
¼ teaspoon sugar
1/8 teaspoon salt
Dash freshly ground black pepper

Mix all ingredients together and pour over salad greens.
Yield: ¾ cup

FRENCH DRESSING

2 tablespoons olive oil
2 teaspoons vinegar

1/8 teaspoon salt
Dash freshly ground pepper

Mix all ingredients well and pour over salad.
Yield: 2 servings
Note: This is the classic dressing for almost all salads. Lemon juice may be substituted for vinegar at any time.

SOUR CREAM DRESSING

1 teaspoon salt
1 teaspoon sugar
Dash freshly ground pepper

1 tablespoon lemon juice
2 tablespoons vinegar
1 cup sour cream

Combine salt, sugar and pepper in a bowl. Add lemon juice, then vinegar. When mixture is smooth, add sour cream and stir well. Chill.
Yield: 1¼ cups
Note: Good dressing for cole slaw—mix with shredded cabbage and sprinkle with paprika. Makes enough dressing for 4 servings of cole slaw.

1 medium cucumber
1 cup mayonnaise

1/8 teaspoon salt
Dash freshly ground pepper

Peel cucumber, cut in half and remove seeds. Cut up coarsely into the blender jar. Whirl at top speed, stopping the power frequently to scrape the cucumber into the center with a rubber spatula. Continue until well pureed. Stir into the mayonnaise. Add salt and pepper; chill, covered, until ready to serve.

Yield: About 1⅓ cups

FRUIT SALAD DRESSING

¼ cup fresh orange juice
1½ teaspoons fresh lemon juice
Dash salt
1 egg, separated

3 tablespoons sugar
2 tablespoons heavy cream, whipped
Grated orange rind for garnish

Cook orange juice in a saucepan over low heat. Beat lemon juice, salt and egg yolk together in the top of a double boiler; gradually beat in 2 tablespoons of the sugar. Slowly stir in hot orange juice. Cook over hot water, stirring constantly, until thickened. Remove from heat. Beat egg white until soft peaks form; gradually beat in remaining tablespoon of sugar. Fold into cooked mixture. Chill. Fold in whipped cream just before serving. Garnish with grated orange rind.

Yield: About 1¼ cups

Desserts

    Whenever you're in the mood for a special hot dessert, turn on your "Mac" fast cooker and whip up a crepe or pancake finish to your meal. Or perhaps you'd prefer a fruit fritter. It's so easy to satisfy your sweet desires—no need to save dessert for company meals, when you cook and clean up in a jiffy.

¼ teaspoon salt
2 eggs
⅔ cup flour
2 tablespoons sugar

1 cup milk
2½ tablespoons melted butter
Butter

Place salt in a bowl. Break in eggs and beat with a wire whisk. Add flour and sugar and mix well. Add milk and melted butter; beat thoroughly. Strain. The batter should be the consistency of thick cream. Allow to rest at least an hour before using. Heat open "Double Mac" grill 5 minutes. Butter it lightly. Place a scant tablespoon of batter on each side of the grill, taking care that the two crepes do not meet in the center. Cook about 1 minute. Turn the crepes and cook about ½ minute on second side. They will be browned in a spotty fashion, which will be used for the inside of the finished crepe. Crepes may be made ahead, refrigerated and reheated when needed.

Yield: About 10 4" crepes
Note: If using "Little Mac" cook one at a time.

FILLINGS FOR DESSERT CREPES

Jam or jelly
Fresh fruits [berries or sliced larger fruits]
Stewed fruits
Orange marmalade [heat and sprinkle with grated orange rind and a dash of cinnamon]
Note: When ready to use, stuff crepes and reheat in butter on the "Mac" grill for about 1 minute. Sprinkle with Verifine sugar before serving.

2 small bananas
2 tablespoons butter
2 tablespoons brown sugar

Dash cinnamon
2 ounces dark rum

Peel bananas and cut in half crosswise. Cut each half into four lengthwise pieces. Heat open "Double Mac" grill 5 minutes. Melt butter in it. Place banana pieces in butter and sprinkle with brown sugar and cinnamon. Saute until lightly browned, about 2 minutes. Turn and saute second side. Meanwhile warm the rum. When bananas are done, pour warm rum over them and ignite.

Yield: 2-3 servings

Note: If using "Little Mac" cook half at a time.

PEACH FRITTERS

2 ripe peaches
1 tablespoon sugar
1 tablespoon Kirsch
½ cup flour
2 teaspoons sugar
1½ teaspoons melted butter

Water
1 egg, beaten
Dash of salt
Butter
Superfine sugar

Peel peaches and cut in half, discarding pits. Cut each half into 3 or 4 pieces. Place in a bowl and sprinkle lightly with 1 tablespoon sugar and Kirsch. Let stand 30 minutes. Drain off the juice formed by the peaches and Kirsch; add enough water to measure ¼ cup. Dry the peach slices on paper toweling. Sift flour and sugar into a bowl and stir in melted butter. Add peach liquid. Mix in egg and salt. The batter should be the consistency of thick cream; if it is too thick, add a little more Kirsch. Dip peach slices into the batter. Heat open "Mac" grill 5 minutes. Add butter; when it melts, put in a few fritters and fry to golden on both sides, about 2-3 minutes, adding more butter if needed. Finish the remaining fritters, sprinkle all with superfine sugar and serve at once.

Yield: 2-3 servings

1½ cups cooked rice

3 egg yolks

½ cup mixed candied fruits,
chopped fine

2 tablespoons Kirsch

Flour

1 egg, beaten

2 tablespoons milk

Ground blanched almonds

Butter

Mix rice with egg yolks in a saucepan. Cook over low heat, stirring constantly, until it thickens and leaves the sides of the pan. Remove from heat and
stir in candied fruits and Kirsch. Spread mixture in a shallow pan and chill.
When ready to serve, form rice mixture into small cakes, dredge with flour,
dip into beaten egg and milk. Then coat with almonds. Heat open "Double
Mac" grill 5 minutes. Add butter; when melted, add rice cakes and cook until
browned on one side. Turn and brown second side, adding more butter if
needed. Serve with Zabaglione Sauce below.

Yield: 2-3 servings

Note: If using "Little Mac" cook one at a time.

ZABAGLIONE SAUCE

3 egg yolks

2 tablespoons sugar

½ cup Marsala wine

Mix together egg yolks and sugar. Add wine and put into the top of a double
boiler over hot water. Beat slowly and steadily with a wire whisk until mixture
thickens. Serve hot over rice cakes or almost any fruit dessert.

Yield: 1 cup

1 medium-size firm banana
1 egg, beaten
2 tablespoons dark rum

Grated pecans or walnuts
Butter

Peel banana and cut it into 1"-wide slices. Combine eggs and rum. Dip each slice in egg mixture. Roll in grated nuts. Heat open "Double Mac" grill 5 minutes. Melt 1 tablespoon butter on it. Put in banana pieces. Cook until nicely browned, about 2 minutes. Turn and brown the other side, adding more butter if needed. Serve hot, sprinkled with Verifine sugar.

Yield: 2 servings

Note: If using "Little Mac" cook in two batches.

LITTLE DESSERT SANDWICHES

4 slices white bread
Jam or jelly

Butter

Spread two slices of bread with jelly or jam. Cover with remaining slices. Cut each sandwich into four quarters. Heat open "Double Mac" grill 5 minutes. Melt 1 tablespoon butter on it. Put in sandwiches. Cook until underside is browned to your taste, about 1 minute. Turn and brown the other side, about 1 minute. Serve hot with Custard Sauce, below, or sweetened whipped cream.

Yield: 2 servings

Note: If using "Little Mac" cook 4 pieces at a time.

CUSTARD SAUCE

1 egg, slightly beaten
Dash salt
2 teaspoons sugar

1 cup milk, scalded
¼ teaspoon vanilla

Combine egg, salt and sugar in the top of a double boiler. Gradually add hot milk, stirring constantly. Cook over boiling water, stirring constantly, until mixture coats a metal spoon. Add vanilla and cool quickly.

Yield: About 1 cup

½ cup plus 1 tablespoon flour
1½ teaspoons sugar
Dash salt
¼ cup beer

1 egg white, beaten stiff
1 apple
½ cup peanut oil
Cinnamon sugar

Mix flour, sugar and salt. Add beer. Fold in egg white. Let stand about 6 hours in a warm (not hot) place before using. Peel apple and cut into slices about ½'' thick. Coat these with the batter, which is quite thick. Heat open "Mac" grill 5 minutes. Add oil; when hot, fry beignets a few at a time so that they do not touch and stick together, until golden on one side, about 3 minutes. Turn and fry the other side until golden, 2-3 minutes. Drain on paper toweling and keep warm until all are finished. Sprinkle with cinnamon sugar. Serve with Vanilla Sauce below, if desired.
Yield: 2 servings

VANILLA SAUCE

1 egg yolk
1 tablespoon sugar
Dash salt

½ teaspoon vanilla
½ cup boiling milk

Heat all ingredients together, beating constantly until thickened. Serve hot, pouring around the beignets.
Yield: About ½ cup

This dish is popular in the Netherlands—the Dutch call it "Sop."

2 slices white bread,
crusts removed
1 egg
⅔ cup milk

¼ teaspoon vanilla
Butter
Cinammon-sugar

Place slices of bread in a shallow dish. Beat egg with milk and vanilla; pour over bread. Allow to soak ½ to ¾ hour. Heat open "Double Mac" grill 5 minutes. Add butter generously. When it melts, put in bread slices and cook until bottoms are golden, about 2 minutes. Turn and brown the second side, adding more butter if needed.

Yield: 2 servings
Note: If using "Little Mac" cook one at a time.

2 thick slices pound cake
1 tablespoon butter

Topping*

Heat open "Double Mac" grill 5 minutes. Add butter; when melted, put in pound cake slices. Cook 1 minute to brown to golden. Turn, adding more butter if needed, and cook 1 minute more to brown second side.

Yield: 2 servings
Note: If using "Little Mac" cook one at a time.

*Suggested Toppings

Chocolate sauce; ice cream; hot maple syrup; fresh fruit; canned fruit; whipped cream seasoned with sugar and vanilla and sprinkled with shaved bitter chocolate.

1 MacIntosh apple	**1 tablespoon brown sugar**
1 tablespoon butter	**Dash of cinnamon**

Peel and core apple. Cut it into halves and cut each half into four slices. Heat open "Double Mac" grill 5 minutes. Melt butter on it. Put in apple pieces and cook, stirring and turning with a wooden spatula until lightly browned, about 2 minutes. Do not let the pieces get too soft or mushy. Sprinkle with the sugar. Stir briefly and constantly with a wooden spatula for about ½ minute, so that the sugar melts and partially coats each apple slice. Be careful not to burn sugar. Sprinkle with cinnamon and serve at once.

Yield: 2 servings

Note: If using "Little Mac" cook only two at a time. Additional butter and brown sugar will be needed.

KISERSCHMARRN

The story goes that the raisins added to a simple pancake make it a dish for the Kaiser.

3 eggs	**1 teaspoon sugar**
¾ cup flour	**¼ cup white raisins**
1 cup milk	**Butter**
¼ teaspoon salt	

Beat eggs lightly. Add flour and mix well. Add milk gradually, beating very thoroughly, and adding just enough to make a thin pancake consistency. Add salt, sugar and raisins. Heat open "Double Mac" grill 5 minutes. Melt butter on it. Fry pancakes until golden brown on the bottom, about 2 minutes. Turn and brown the other side to golden. Repeat. Cut each pancake into long thin strips, sprinkle with Verifine sugar and serve at once on hot plates.

Yield: 4 servings

Note: If using "Little Mac" cook one at a time.

3 eggs, separated

3 tablespoons lemon juice

Grated rind of 1 lemon

3 tablespoons sugar

½ teaspoon salt

¼ teaspoon nutmeg

1 cup milk

1 cup sifted cake flour

Butter

Cinnamon-sugar

Separate eggs. Beat yolks; add remainder of ingredients, except egg whites and butter. Beat smooth. Beat egg whites until stiff peaks form; fold into batter. Heat open "Double Mac" grill 5 minutes and butter lightly. Fry two pancakes at a time, about 2 minutes on each side, or until golden, adding butter for each new lot. Serve sprinkled with cinnamon-sugar.

Yield: 4 servings

Note: If using "Little Mac" cook one at a time.

POFFERTJES

This is one of the most typical and delicious of Dutch desserts—usually cooked in a special pan that produces a ball shape. The same batter can be cooked as a light and airy pancake.

1 cup plus 2 tablespoons flour

3 egg yolks

½ cup milk

½ cup beer

Butter

Mix together flour, egg yolks, milk and beer. The beer causes the mixture to rise instantly. Heat the open "Double Mac" grill 5 minutes. Butter it well. Place about a tablespoon of batter for each poffertje on the grill. When the first side is golden, about 1 minute, turn and brown the other side. Repeat. Serve with melted butter and Verifine sugar sprinkled over them.

Yield: 2-3 servings

Note: If using "Little Mac" cook two at a time.

CREPES AU BANANA

2 small ripe bananas
1 egg, separated
1 teaspoon brown sugar
Grated rind of ¼ lemon

1 tablespoon flour
¼ teaspoon salt
Juice of ½ lemon
2 tablespoons milk

Peel bananas and mash them with a fork until reduced to a pulp. Beat them until creamy. Add egg yolk, sugar, lemon rind, flour, salt, lemon juice and milk. When well mixed, beat egg white stiff and fold it in. Batter should be like thin sour cream. If it is too thick add a little milk. Heat open "Double Mac" grill 5 minutes. Butter it well. Fry pancakes in butter on both sides until golden. Serve sprinkled with Verifine sugar and more lemon juice.
Yield: 2 servings
Note: If using "Little Mac" cook one at a time.

DUTCH PANCAKES

5 eggs, separated
½ cup sugar
Grated rind of ½ lemon
¼ teaspoon powdered cloves

½ cup half-and-half cream
¾ cup flour
Dash salt
1 cup apricot jam

Beat egg yolks with sugar until creamy and light. Add lemon rind, cloves, cream, flour and salt. Beat well and add stiffly beaten egg whites. Set aside for 15 minutes. Heat open "Double Mac" grill 5 minutes; butter it well. Make pancakes about 1/8" thick, browning to golden on the bottom, then turning to brown the second sides, 2-3 minutes in all. Spread with jam and roll up. Sprinkle with Verifine sugar and serve hot. Repeat until all batter is cooked.
Yield: 4 servings
Note: If using "Little Mac" cook one at a time.

Deep Fryer Cooking

Time was when deep frying was a session of spattering fat and messy cleanups afterward. No more. The "Fry All" deep fryer has it all under control. Just two and one-half cups of oil in a miraculous little unit that can cook and store with a minimum of effort and a maximum of enjoyment. There's something for every meal in this recipe section. Try it and see how crispy-crunchy freshly fried foods can be!

If you thought your "Fry All" was only for frying, you're in for a delightful surprise. Just try it for grilling hot dogs, hamburgers or steaks, or for heating soups and vegetables.

TO BOIL, COOK & HEAT
1. Make sure "Fry All" is clean and empty.
2. Add desired amount of water.
3. Basket may be used for cooking and draining boiled food.
4. Attach plug to unit first, then plug into wall outlet. The unit is on and will remain that way until unplugged.
5. Boil water.
6. Add desired amount of food.
Note: Maximum usable volume of food and water should not exceed five cups.

SOUTHERN FRIED CHICKEN

2½ cups cooking oil
1 frying chicken, about 3 pounds,
    cut up
1 egg, beaten

½ cup milk
1 cup flour
½ teaspoon salt
½ teaspoon paprika

Dip each chicken part into beaten egg mixed with milk. Then dip into mixture of flour, salt and paprika; coat well. Heat oil in "Fry All". Deep fry in hot fat until golden brown, turning chicken frequently. Drain in basket hooked on base. Repeat until all are fried.
Yield: 4 servings

SOUTHERN FRIED CUSTARD

Here's an old-fashioned southern recipe to be served with fried chicken. If custard is chilled firmly you'll get a hot-and-cold sensation.

2 cups milk
3 tablespoons cornstarch
½ cup sugar
3 eggs, separated

¼ teaspoon cinnamon
1 teaspoon vanilla
¼ cup finely ground peanuts
2½ cups cooking oil

Scald milk. Remove from heat; stir in cornstarch, sugar, egg yolks, cinnamon and vanilla. Refrigerate egg whites for later use. Return mixture to heat; cook and stir until thickened. Pour into a greased flat pan; chill overnight. Cut into cubes. Beat egg whites until stiff peaks form. Roll each cube into a small amount of egg whites, forming a ball; roll in ground nuts. Heat oil in "Fry All". Drop a few balls at a time into hot fat and cook until golden brown. Drain in basket hooked on base. Repeat until all are done.
Yield: 6 to 8 servings

4 tablespoons butter
½ teaspoon garlic powder
1 teaspoon minced parsley
1 large chicken breast, split,
    skinned and boned

1 egg
¼ cup flour
¼ cup fine breadcrumbs
2½ cups cooking oil

Combine butter, garlic powder and minced parsley; form into 2 log-shaped rolls. Pound 2 halves of chicken breast flat; insert butter log in natural pocket on underside of each half of chicken. Roll up. Beat egg; dip chicken first in flour, then in egg, and last in breadcrumbs, coating well. Chill for at least 1 hour. Heat oil in "Fry All". Deep fry 15 minutes, or until browned and tender.
Yield: 2 servings

CHICKEN BALLS

2 cups chopped cooked chicken
1 tablespoon grated onion
1 tablespoon minced parsley
1 teaspoon lemon juice
2 tablespoons butter

2 tablespoons flour
1 cup milk
1 egg
½ cup fine breadcrumbs
2½ cups cooking oil

Combine chopped chicken, onion, parsley and lemon juice; set aside. Melt butter in a saucepan; stir in flour until smooth and thick. Remove from heat; gradually stir in milk until smooth. Cook and stir until thickened. Stir sauce into chicken mixture. Chill for several hours. Shape into 1" balls. Beat egg; dip balls in egg and then into breadcrumbs, coating well. Heat oil in "Fry All". Drop a few balls at a time into deep hot fat and cook until golden brown. Remove. Drain in basket hooked on base. Repeat until all are fried. Serve hot.
Yield: About 2 dozen

Are you tired of fussing with your fondue pot? Use your compact "Fry All" instead. Just plug it in and hand out the fondue forks!

2½ cups cooking oil
1 tablespoon freshly squeezed
 lemon juice
1 pound round steak or sirloin tip,
 cut in thin 1-inch strips

½ pound mushrooms, halved
 or quartered
Orange Ginger Sauce [page 152]
Avocado Dill Sauce [page 139]
Blue Cheese Sauce [page 136]

Heat oil in "Fry All". Add lemon juice. Have beef strips and mushrooms at room temperature and place on serving tray on table. Set out small bowls of sauces. Each guest spears a piece of beef or mushroom on a long fondue fork or bamboo skewer, then holds it in the hot oil until cooked to desired doneness, usually 30 to 60 seconds. He then dips it in a sauce on his plate, eating at once. Add more oil to pot as needed and skim surface of oil occasionally.
Yield: 4 servings

Here's the kind of convenience food quick-trick that makes a lot of sense. Nothing to do but coat with egg and coconut—you'll be serving it just minutes later.

2½ cups cooking oil
1 10-ounce package frozen
 breaded shrimp

1 egg, beaten
1 tablespoon water
½ cup shredded coconut

Heat oil in "Fry All". Dip each shrimp into combined egg and water; then roll in shredded coconut. Drop a few into deep hot fat and fry until golden brown. Drain in basket hooked on base. Repeat until all are fried.
Yield: 2 to 4 servings

4 breakfast sausages
2 eggs
1 tablespoon cold water

1/8 teaspoon salt
Dash of pepper

Place sausages in the bottom of oil-free "Fry All". Plug in and cook sausages, turning occasionally. Remove from fryer. Pour off excess fat. Beat two eggs in a bowl; add water, salt and pepper. Pour into the fryer and scramble eggs by gently pushing the solid forming mass to the center of the fryer and allowing the liquid egg to flow to the edges. When all is solidified but still moist, remove and serve with sausages.
Yield: 1 or 2 servings

FRIED PEACH PIES

1 cup flour
¼ teaspoon salt
⅓ cup butter or shortening
2 tablespoons ice water
2 cups fresh peaches, chopped fine
¼ cup sugar
2 tablespoons cornstarch

¼ teaspoon nutmeg
1/8 teaspoon cinnamon
1 teaspoon lemon juice
1 teaspoon butter
2½ cups cooking oil
Confectioners' sugar

Combine flour and salt; cut in butter until the particles are mealy in appearance. Add ice water and work dough until it is a soft ball. Roll out and cut into 3" rounds, using the floured rim of a large glass. In a saucepan, combine peaches, sugar, cornstarch, nutmeg and cinnamon; cook over low heat, stirring constantly, until mixture is thick and clear. Add lemon juice and butter, stirring until butter is melted. Remove from heat and cool. Place mixture on half the circle of dough, fold empty half over and press the edges together; crimp with the tines of a fork. Heat oil in the "Fry All" and drop in several at a time to fry until golden brown. Drain in basket hooked on base. Repeat until all are fried. Serve sprinkled with confectioners' sugar.
Yield: About 1 dozen

The Japanese have a way of dipping small pieces of food in batter and then deep frying into tender morsels of delicate taste. Once you've mastered the technique you'll save odd pieces of fish and vegetables to cook a meal fit for an emperor.

2½ cups cooking oil	1 egg
1 cup flour	1½ pounds medium-size fresh shrimp
1 cup water	Japanese Dipping Sauce [see below]

Heat oil in "Fry All". Combine flour, water and egg, mixing ingredients together lightly. Batter may be lumpy. Remove shells of shrimp, leaving tails intact. Cut down the center of each and flatten into a butterfly shape. Dip each shrimp in batter and drop into the hot fat. Fry until golden brown. Drain in basket hooked on base. Repeat until all are fried. Serve hot with Japanese Dipping Sauce that follows.

Yield: 6 servings

Note: Flounder, filleted smelts or lobster chunks may be substituted for shrimp. The same batter may be used for green pepper (halved, seeded and cut in quarters), carrot (cut in thin slices), broccoli (in small flowerettes), green beans, sweet potato (in thin slices), onion slices, zucchini slices, eggplant (cut in chunks), canned bamboo shoot (sliced), and sliced Belgian endive.

Note II: May be cooked on "Double Mac" grill using ½ cup oil and cooking small quantities at a time. Fry, turning frequently for best results.

JAPANESE DIPPING SAUCE

1 cup dashi* or chicken stock	1 teaspoon grated fresh ginger
⅓ cup mirin [Japanese sweet wine]	⅓ cup grated white daikon radish
⅓ cup light soy sauce	or grated fresh turnip

Mix dashi, mirin and soy sauce. Heat to the boiling point and remove from heat; keep warm. Pour sauce into individual bowls; heap grated radish or turnip in center.

* Dashi is a clear broth made from seaweed and shaved bonito. It can be purchased in dehydrated form in Japanese stores and reconstituted with water.

Yield: 2 cups

½ pound raw shrimp, peeled
    and deveined
1 onion
1 clove garlic, peeled
½ cup Italian-seasoned
    breadcrumbs

1 egg
1 teaspoon Worcestershire sauce
¼ teaspoon salt
1/8 teaspoon pepper
¼ cup flour
2½ cups cooking oil

Chop or grind shrimp, onion and garlic. Add breadcrumbs, egg, Worcestershire sauce, salt and pepper. Form into 1" balls. Roll balls in flour. Chill for at least 1 hour. Heat oil in "Fry All". Deep fry balls a few at a time until golden brown. Drain in basket hooked on base. Repeat.

Yield: 4-6 servings

DEEP-FRIED CUCUMBERS

2 firm cucumbers
¼ cup oil
¼ cup vinegar
1 teaspoon sugar
½ teaspoon salt

1/8 teaspoon pepper
1 egg, beaten
½ cup fine breadcrumbs
2½ cups cooking oil

Peel and slice cucumbers into ¼" rounds. Combine oil, vinegar, sugar, salt and pepper in a flat pan; marinate cucumber slices in this mixture for 10 minutes. Drain. Heat oil in "Fry All". Dip each slice in beaten egg and then in breadcrumbs. Deep fry until golden brown. Remove. Drain in basket hooked on base. Repeat until all are fried.

Yield: 6 servings

DEEP FRIED SCALLOPS

2½ cups cooking oil
1 pound bay scallops
½ cup flour
½ teaspoon salt

1 egg, beaten
1 cup fine breadcrumbs
Lemon slices

Heat oil in "Fry All". Dip each scallop into combined flour and salt, then into egg, then roll in breadcrumbs. Drop a few at a time into deep hot fat and fry until golden brown. Drain in basket hooked on base. Repeat until all are fried. Serve with lemon slices.
Yield: 2 servings

FISH CROQUETTES

2 tablespoons butter
2 tablespoons flour
½ cup milk
1 egg yolk
1½ cups cold cooked fish
1 teaspoon grated onion

1 teaspoon chopped parsley
½ teaspoon salt
½ cup breadcrumbs
1 egg, beaten
2½ cups cooking oil

Melt butter in a saucepan; stir in flour until smooth and thick. Remove from heat. Gradually stir in milk until smooth. Cook and stir until thickened. Remove from heat; add egg yolk, cooked fish, onion, parsley and salt. Chill. Shape mixture into cones; dip in breadcrumbs, then in beaten egg and finally in breadcrumbs again. Heat oil in "Fry All". Deep fry croquettes until browned.
Yield: 4 servings

2½ cups cooking oil
¾ cup shredded crab meat
½ cup milk
1 egg, separated

1 cup flour
¼ teaspoon salt
¼ teaspoon dried dillweed
1/8 teaspoon pepper

Heat oil in "Fry All". Combine crab meat and milk; beat egg yolk and add. Sift flour, salt, dillweed and pepper; stir into crab mixture. Beat egg white until stiff peaks form; fold into crab mixture. Drop by tablespoonsful into deep hot fat; cook until golden brown. Drain in basket hooked on base. Repeat until all batter is cooked. Serve hot.

Yield: About 1 dozen fritters

PARSLEY PUFFS

2½ cups cooking oil
1 egg
¼ cup water
½ cup flour

1½ teaspoons cornstarch
½ teaspoon baking powder
½ teaspoon onion salt
3 cups fresh parsley sprigs

Heat oil in "Fry All". Beat egg until fluffy; add water. Add flour, cornstarch, baking powder and onion salt. Dip parsley sprigs into batter, one at a time, letting excess batter drip back into bowl. Drop several sprigs at a time into hot oil; remove when golden brown and drain in basket hooked on base. Repeat. Serve hot.

Yield: 6-8 servings

2½ cups cooking oil
1½ cups ground clams
¼ cup clam liquor
1 cup milk
2 eggs, separated

2 cups flour
½ teaspoon salt
½ teaspoon ginger
1/8 teaspoon pepper

Heat oil in "Fry All". Combine clams, clam liquor and milk. Beat egg yolks and add to clams. Sift flour, salt, ginger and pepper; stir into clam mixture. Beat egg whites until stiff peaks form. Fold egg whites into clam mixture. Drop by tablespoonsful into deep hot fat; cook until golden brown. Drain in basket hooked on base. Repeat until all batter is cooked. Serve hot.

Yield: About 2 dozen fritters

RICE CROQUETTES

The secret of making good croquettes is to chill the mixture thoroughly before deep frying. That way it holds its shape while crisping well on the outside.

1 cup leftover boiled rice
1 egg, beaten
1 teaspoon sugar
1 teaspoon melted butter
¼ teaspoon salt

2 tablespoons heavy cream
1 egg, beaten
½ cup fine breadcrumbs
2½ cups cooking oil

Combine boiled rice, 1 beaten egg, sugar, melted butter, salt and cream; mix well. Add additional cream if needed to make mixture easy to form into 1½" balls. Dip balls into remaining beaten egg and then into breadcrumbs, coating well. Chill for at least one hour. Heat oil in "Fry All". Drop several balls at a time into hot oil and fry until golden brown. Drain in basket hooked on base. Repeat until all are fried.

Yield: 4 servings

DEEP FRIED OYSTERS

2½ cups cooking oil
1 cup dry pancake mix
1 pint shucked oysters, drained

½ teaspoon salt
Cocktail sauce or Sauce Tartare

Heat oil in "Fry All". Put pancake mix into large shallow bowl. Add oysters, a few at a time, and toss lightly until well coated. Shake off excess breading. Fry in deep fat until golden brown, 1½-2 minutes. Drain in basket hooked on base. Repeat process until all oysters are cooked. Salt lightly and serve with cocktail sauce or Sauce Tartare (page 92).
Yield: 4 servings

FRENCH-FRIED ZUCCHINI

2½ cups cooking oil
1 egg
¼ cup water
½ cup flour

1½ teaspoons cornstarch
½ teaspoon baking powder
1 teaspoon garlic powder
2 zucchini, cut into "French-fry" strips

Heat oil in "Fry All". Beat egg until fluffy; add water. Add flour, cornstarch, baking powder and garlic powder. Dip zucchini strips into batter, one at a time, letting excess batter drop back into bowl. Drop several zucchini strips at a time into hot oil; remove when golden brown and drain in basket hooked on base. Repeat. Serve hot.
Yield: 6 to 8 servings

OMELET

2 eggs
2 tablespoons water
¼ teaspoon salt

Pinch pepper
1½ tablespoons butter or margarine

Beat eggs with water, salt and pepper until just blended. Melt butter in preheated "Fry All". Pour in eggs. As mixture sets at edge, with fork, draw this portion toward center so that uncooked portions flow to bottom. Tilt "Fry All" as necessary to hasten flow of uncooked eggs to bottom. When eggs are set and surface is still moist, with spatula, loosen edge of omelet all around, and carefully roll up omelet toward opposite side. Hold "Fry All" handle and tip until omelet rolls out on platter.

Yield: 1 serving

BLUE CHEESE SAUCE

1 tablespoon crumbled blue cheese
1 tablespoon orange juice
1 teaspoon freshly grated
    orange rind

½ cup catsup
1/8 teaspoon Worcestershire sauce
¼ teaspoon grated horseradish

Mash blue cheese with orange juice. Add remaining ingredients and blend thoroughly. Allow to stand at least 1 hour before serving.

Yield: About ¾ cup sauce

MUSTARD DIP

½ cup prepared mustard
2 tablespoons salad oil
2 tablespoons wine vinegar

½ cup mayonnaise
1 teaspoon chopped chives

Stir all ingredients together until well blended. Refrigerate for several hours or overnight.

Yield: 1¼ cups

CHICKEN SOUP AMANDINE

1 can condensed cream of
   chicken soup
1 soup can milk
2 tablespoons finely chopped
   blanched almonds

1 teaspoon chopped parsley
1 drop Tabasco
Pinch of ground cloves
Pinch of ground nutmeg

Empty soup into a clean dry "Fry All". Add milk, mix well. Plug in fryer. Add remaining ingredients. Heat until thoroughly hot.
Yield: 2-3 servings

GREEN PEPPER RINGS

2½ cups cooking oil
1 egg
¼ cup water
½ cup flour

1½ teaspoons cornstarch
½ teaspoon baking powder
2 large green peppers, seeded
   and cut in ¼" rings

Heat oil in "Fry All". Beat egg until fluffy; add water. Add flour, cornstarch and baking powder. Dip pepper rings into batter, one at a time, letting excess batter drip back into bowl. Drop several rings at a time into hot oil; remove when golden brown and drain in basket hooked on base. Repeat. Serve hot.
Yield: 6 servings

DILL DIP

1½ cups mayonnaise
½ cup dairy sour cream
3 tablespoons finely chopped fresh dill

¼ teaspoon grated onion
2 teaspoons chopped chives

Combine mayonnaise and sour cream; add fresh dill. (If you must substitute, use 1 teaspoon dried dill.) Add onion and chives. Mix well and chill.
Yield: 2¼ cups

1 can condensed cream of
   mushroom soup
1 cup milk
1 can [7¾-ounces] salmon,
   including liquid

¼ teaspoon ground pepper
½ teaspoon paprika
¼ cup sherry wine, optional
1 teaspoon lemon juice

Empty soup into a clean, dry "Fry All". Add milk and mix well. Plug in fryer. Break salmon into small pieces while in the can and remove any visible bones; mix into the soup. Add remaining ingredients. Heat through.
Yield: 2-3 servings

MINTED CARROTS AND WAX BEANS

1 can [16 ounces] carrot slices
1 can [16 ounces] cut wax beans
1 tablespoon butter

1 teaspoon lemon juice
½ teaspoon chopped dried mint leaves

Preheat clean and dry "Fry All" for 5 minutes. Empty juice from cans of carrots and wax beans into it and cook to reduce volume of liquid to about half. Add butter, lemon juice and mint; heat until butter melts. Add carrot slices and cut wax beans; heat through.
Yield: 6 servings

GREEN BEANS ORIENTAL

2 tablespoons peanut oil
2 packages [10 ounces each] frozen
   French cut green beans
1 small onion, cut in thin slivers

¼ cup soy sauce
1 cup slivered toasted almonds
Dash of pepper

Heat peanut oil in the bottom of the "Fry All". Add beans and slivered onions; cook until hot, stirring occasionally. Add soy sauce, almonds and pepper; mix well.
Yield: 6 servings

MUSHROOM CAPS

2½ cups cooking oil
1 egg
¼ cup water
½ cup flour

1½ teaspoons cornstarch
½ teaspoon baking powder
1 teaspoon Parmesan cheese
1 pound medium mushroom caps

Heat oil in "Fry All". Beat eggs until fluffy; add water. Add flour, cornstarch, baking powder and Parmesan cheese. Dip mushroom caps into batter, one at a time, letting excess batter drip back into bowl. Drop several mushroom caps at a time into hot oil; remove when golden brown and drain in basket hooked on base. Repeat. Serve hot.
Yield: 6 to 8 servings

AVOCADO DIP

2 very ripe avocados
2 drops Tabasco
½ teaspoon salt

2 teaspoons lemon juice
2 tablespoons white horseradish
½ cup dairy sour cream

Mash avocados. Add Tabasco. Stir in salt, lemon juice, horseradish, sour cream. Mix well and chill for at least 1 hour.
Yield: About 1¼ cups

AVOCADO DILL SAUCE

½ ripe avocado, mashed
¼ teaspoon freshly grated
  lemon rind
1 teaspoon lemon juice

½ cup dairy sour cream
½ teaspoon seasoned salt
1/8 teaspoon dried dill weed,
  or more to taste

Combine avocado with lemon rind and juice. Blend in remaining ingredients. Chill.
Yield: About ¾ cup sauce

Does it pay to make your own potato chips? Certainly, if you like them super fresh and paper thin!

4 large potatoes   **2½ cups cooking oil**
Cold salted water

Pare potatoes and wash; slice very thin. Soak in cold salted water for several minutes. Drain and dry well. Heat oil in "Fry All". Fry a few at a time in deep fat until golden brown. Remove and drain in basket hooked on base. Repeat. Sprinkle with salt and serve hot or cold.
Yield: 4 to 6 servings
Note: Serve with the recipes for Dill Dip (page 137), Mustard Dip (page 136) or Avocado Dip (page 139).

FRENCH-FRIED CAULIFLOWER

2½ cups cooking oil   **¼ teaspoon salt**
1 egg yolk, beaten   **1/8 teaspoon pepper**
½ cup milk   **1 head cauliflower, broken into**
½ cup flour   **flowerets**
1 teaspoon baking powder

Heat oil in "Fry All". Combine egg yolk and milk; add flour, baking powder, salt and pepper. Beat until smooth. Dip pieces of cauliflower into batter, letting excess drip off. Drop into deep fat and fry until golden brown. Remove and drain in basket hooked on base. Repeat until all are fried.
Yield: 6 servings

4 large potatoes   2½ cups cooking oil
Cold salted water

Pare, wash and cut potatoes into long strips. Soak in cold salted water for several minutes. Drain and dry well. Heat oil in "Fry All". Drop a portion of the potatoes into the deep hot fat and cook until golden. Remove and drain in basket hooked on base. Repeat until all are cooked. Sprinkle with salt and serve hot.

Yield: 4 servings

EGGPLANT CUBES PARMIGIANA

2½ cups cooking oil   ½ teaspoon baking powder
1 egg   2 tablespoons grated Parmesan cheese
¼ cup water   1 medium eggplant, peeled and
½ cup flour   cut into ¾" cubes
1½ teaspoons cornstarch

Heat oil in "Fry All". Beat egg until fluffy; add water. Add flour, cornstarch, baking powder and Parmesan cheese. Dip eggplant cubes into batter, one at a time, letting excess batter drip back into bowl. Drop several cubes at a time into hot oil; remove when golden brown and drain in basket hooked on base. Repeat. Serve hot.

Yield: 6 to 8 servings

FRIED OKRA

2½ cups cooking oil   ½ teaspoon salt
2 cups fresh okra   ¼ teaspoon pepper
¼ cup flour

Heat oil in "Fry All". Slice okra across the pod into small pieces. Combine flour, salt and pepper in a small bag; shake okra in bag until well coated. Drop several pieces at a time into deep hot fat until browned. Drain in basket hooked on base. Repeat until all are fried.

Yield: 4 to 6 servings

6 eggs, separated
3 cups cooked kernel corn
   [may be canned]
1½ teaspoons salt

1 teaspoon Tabasco
½ cup flour
2½ cups cooking oil

Beat egg yolks until light. Mix in corn, salt, Tabasco and flour. Beat egg whites until stiff but not dry; fold into corn mixture. Heat oil in "Fry All". Drop some of mixture by tablespoon into hot oil. Cook for several minutes until golden brown. Remove and drain in basket hooked on base. Repeat with remaining batter.

Yield: 8 to 12 servings

TOMATO FRITTERS

2½ cups cooking oil
1 cup flour
1 cup water
1 tablespoon butter, melted

½ teaspoon salt
1 egg white, beaten stiff
4 large tomatoes, cut into
   thick slices

Heat oil in "Fry All". Combine flour, water, melted butter and salt. Fold stiffly beaten egg white into flour mixture. Dip slices of tomato into batter and deep fry until golden brown. Drain in basket hooked on base. Repeat until all slices are browned.

Yield: 4 to 6 servings

2½ cups cooking oil
1 egg
¼ cup water
½ cup flour

1½ teaspoons cornstarch
½ teaspoon baking powder
1 teaspoon garlic powder
1 pound whole green beans, trimmed

Heat oil in "Fry All". Beat egg until fluffy; add water. Add flour, cornstarch, baking powder and garlic powder. Dip green beans into batter, one at a time, letting excess batter drip back into bowl. Drop several beans at a time into hot oil; remove when golden brown and drain in basket hooked on base. Repeat. Serve hot.
Yield: 6 to 8 servings

2½ cups cooking oil
1 12-ounce package corn bread mix
1 tablespoon dehydrated minced onion

1 egg
⅓ cup beer

Heat oil in "Fry All". Combine corn bread mix, onion, egg and beer. Stir together until well blended. Drop by scant tablespoonsful into deep hot oil and fry for several minutes until golden brown. Drain in basket hooked on base. Repeat until all are done. Serve hot.
Yield: About 2 dozen

3 cups water
1 package [10 ounces] mixed vegetables frozen in butter sauce
  in boil-in-bag plastic pouch

2 tablespoons slivered almonds
¼ teaspoon salt
Dash of pepper

Pour water into clean, dry "Fry All". Plug in and heat to boiling. Slip pouch of mixed vegetables into boiling water. Bring water to second boil; continue cooking about 14 minutes. Remove; empty contents into a bowl. Add almonds, salt and pepper.
Yield: 2-3 servings

SWEET POTATO MARSHMALLOW BALLS

3 cups mashed cooked
  sweet potatoes
1 tablespoon butter
1 tablespoon brown sugar
½ teaspoon salt

12 marshmallows, cut in half
1 egg
1 cup chopped pecans
2½ cups cooking oil

Combine sweet potatoes, butter, brown sugar and salt; wrap about 2 tablespoons of mixture around each piece of marshmallow, forming a ball. Beat egg. Dip balls in egg and then in chopped pecans. Refrigerate for at least 1 hour. Heat oil in "Fry All". Drop several balls into deep hot fat and fry until golden brown. Drain in basket hooked on base. Repeat.
Yield: 24 balls

2 large Bermuda onions
1 cup milk
½ cup flour

½ teaspoon salt
2½ cups cooking oil

Slice onion into ¼"-thick rings. Separate rings and soak in milk for at least 20 minutes. Drain. Combine flour and salt in a small bag; shake onion rings in bag until well coated. Heat oil in "Fry All". Drop several onion rings at a time into deep hot fat until golden brown. Drain in basket hooked on base. Repeat until all are fried.

Yield: 4 to 6 servings

SWEET POTATO CROQUETTES

3 cups mashed cooked
    sweet potatoes
2 eggs
1 tablespoon brown sugar

2 tablespoons butter
½ teaspoon salt
1 cup fine breadcrumbs
2½ cups cooking oil

Combine mashed sweet potatoes with 1 egg; add brown sugar, butter and salt. Mix well. Form into balls. Beat remaining egg. Dip balls into breadcrumbs, then into egg and again into crumbs, coating well. Chill for at least 1 hour. Heat oil in "Fry All". Deep fry several potato balls at a time until golden brown. Drain in basket hooked on base.

Yield: 6 servings

2½ cups cooking oil
2 cups sifted cornmeal
1 egg
2 teaspoons baking powder
¼ cup buttermilk

1½ cups water
1 teaspoon sugar
½ teaspoon salt
2 tablespoons grated onion

Heat oil in "Fry All". Combine cornmeal, egg, baking powder, buttermilk and water; mix well. Add sugar, salt and grated onion. Drop by teaspoonsful into deep hot fat; fry until golden brown. Drain in basket hooked on base. Repeat until all batter is used. Serve hot.

Yield: 6 servings

POTATO PUFFS

1 cup hot cooked mashed potatoes
4 tablespoons butter
1 egg, beaten
1 tablespoon grated onion

½ cup flour
1 teaspoon baking powder
¼ teaspoon salt
2½ cups cooking oil

Combine hot mashed potatoes with butter until butter is melted through. Add egg, onion, flour, baking powder and salt. Chill. Heat oil in "Fry All". Drop by teaspoonsful into deep hot fat and fry until golden. Drain in basket hooked on base. Repeat until all are fried.

Yield: 4 servings

This pastry, with a surprise bit of mushroom filling, fries up soft and delectable. Can be frozen before cooking—just reach into the freezer and pop into hot fat.

Pastry

½ **cup butter**
4 ounces cream cheese

1½ **cups flour**
½ **teaspoon salt**

Filling

4 tablespoons butter
½ **pound chopped fresh mushrooms**
1 large onion, cut fine
½ **teaspoon salt**

¼ **teaspoon pepper**
1 tablespoon flour
2½ **cups cooking oil**

Work butter, cream cheese, flour and salt into a smooth dough; roll out and cut in circles with a drinking glass. Prepare filling by melting butter in a skillet; saute mushrooms and onion until limp. Add salt, pepper and flour; stir until mixture is thickened. Cool. Place mixture on half the circle of dough, fold empty half over and press the edges together; crimp with the tines of a fork. Heat 2½ cups cooking oil in the "Fry All" and drop in several at a time to fry until golden brown. Remove and drain in basket hooked at base. Repeat until all are fried. Serve hot.

Yield: About 2 dozen turnovers

COCKTAIL FRANKS WITH APRICOT DIP

2½ **cups cooking oil**
24 cocktail frankfurters

1 cup apricot jam
2 tablespoons prepared mustard

Heat oil in "Fry All". Drop 8 cocktail frankfurters into hot oil for 2 minutes. Remove and drain in basket hooked on base. Repeat. Spear each one with a pick. Keep warm. Combine apricot jam and mustard in a small bowl. Use as dip for the cocktail frankfurters.

Yield: 8 servings

No need to make pastry dough for this one—just dip in batter and deep fry. Cocktail franks will be covered with a luscious coating.

2½ cups cooking oil
½ cup water
¾ cup pancake mix

½ teaspoon salt
½ pound cocktail frankfurters

Heat oil in "Fry All". Combine water, pancake mix and salt. Dip frankfurter into mixture to coat well, letting excess drip off. Deep fry a few at a time until golden brown. Serve with mustard.
Yield: 4 to 6 servings

If you're in the habit of cooking grits for breakfast, cook a little extra and combine with peanuts for an interesting cocktail offering.

1 tablespoon butter
1 tablespoon flour
½ cup milk
¼ teaspoon salt
1 cup cooked salted grits

½ cup chopped peanuts
1 egg
¼ cup fine breadcrumbs
2½ cups cooking oil

Melt butter in a saucepan; stir in flour until bubbly. Remove from heat; gradually stir in milk until smooth. Cook and stir until thickened. Combine with cooked grits and peanuts. Chill well. Form into 1" balls. Beat egg. Dip balls first into breadcrumbs, then into egg, and then again into breadcrumbs, coating well. Chill again. Heat oil in "Fry All". Deep fry balls several at a time until golden brown. Remove and drain in basket hooked on base. Repeat.
Yield: 6 to 8 servings

POTATO DOUGHNUTS

Doughnuts are a natural to make in a deep fryer and you have the satisfaction of knowing there are no preservatives added. Just drop a few at a time in deep hot fat, cook several minutes and drain dry. Mmmm delicious!

1½ **cups flour**
1½ **teaspoons baking powder**
¼ **teaspoon baking soda**
½ **teaspoon salt**
1/8 **teaspoon nutmeg**
1 **egg**

⅓ **cup sugar**
1 **tablespoon melted butter**
1 **cup mashed potato**
¼ **cup buttermilk**
2½ **cups cooking oil**

Sift together flour, baking powder, baking soda, salt and nutmeg. Beat egg; add sugar, butter, mashed potato and buttermilk. Beat well. Stir in dry ingredients. Knead dough lightly; roll into a thin sheet. Cut into rounds with floured rim of a glass. Heat oil in "Fry All". Drop doughnuts in a few at a time and fry until golden brown. Remove. Drain in basket hooked at base. Repeat until all are fried. Serve warm.
Yield: About 1 dozen

RICOTTA CHEESE BALLS

½ **ounce brandy**
½ **pound ricotta cheese**
1 **egg, beaten**
1/8 **teaspoon salt**

¼ **cup flour**
2½ **cups cooking oil**
Confectioners' sugar

Mix the brandy into the cheese with a fork. Add beaten egg. Add salt and flour, mixing thoroughly. Chill for several hours. Heat oil in "Fry All". Drop by teaspoonsful into deep hot oil, a few at a time. When browned they will bob up to the surface. Remove and drain in basket hooked on base. Repeat until all are fried. Cool slightly and sprinkle with confectioners' sugar.
Yield: 1 dozen

2½ cups cooking oil
2 cups sifted flour
¼ cup sugar
1 tablespoon baking powder
1 teaspoon salt

1 teaspoon cinnamon
1 egg
¾ cup milk
¼ cup melted butter
Confectioners' sugar

Heat oil in "Fry All". Combine flour, sugar, baking powder, salt and cinnamon. Beat egg; add milk and melted butter. Stir egg mixture into flour mixture; mix until smooth. Drop by teaspoonsful into hot fat. Cook until golden brown, about 3 minutes. Drain in basket hooked to base. Repeat until all the batter is cooked. Sprinkle with confectioners' sugar.

Yield: About 3 dozen

2½ cups cooking oil
½ cup flour
¾ teaspoon baking powder
¼ teaspoon salt
1/8 teaspoon nutmeg

1 egg
¼ cup milk
1 cup well-drained canned pineapple
    cubes
Confectioners' sugar

Heat oil in "Fry All". Sift flour, baking powder, salt and nutmeg together. Beat egg and milk together; add sifted ingredients. Dip pineapple cubes into batter and then drop into cooking oil to fry until golden; make several at a time. Drain in basket hooked on base. Repeat until all are fried. Sprinkle with confectioners' sugar. Serve warm.

Yield: 2 to 4 servings

2½ cups cooking oil
1 cup grated Swiss cheese
1 cup fine breadcrumbs

½ teaspoon salt
1/8 teaspoon cayenne pepper
2 egg whites

Heat oil in "Fry All". Combine grated cheese with ¾ cup of the bread-crumbs; add salt and cayenne pepper. Beat egg whites stiff; add to cheese. Form 1" balls; coat with remaining ¼ cup breadcrumbs. Drop a few at a time into deep hot fat and fry until golden. Repeat. Drain in basket hooked on base. Serve hot.
Yield: 6-8 servings

2½ cups cooking oil
1 cup grated Cheddar cheese
2 tablespoons flour
½ teaspoon chili powder

½ teaspoon salt
¼ teaspoon pepper
1 egg white
½ cup finely chopped walnuts or
    pecans

Heat oil in "Fry All". Combine cheese, flour, chili powder, salt and pep-per. Beat egg white until stiff peaks form; fold into cheese mixture. Form into 1" balls; roll in nuts to coat evenly. Drop a few at a time into hot fat; cook until golden brown. Remove and drain in basket hooked to base. Repeat.
Yield: About 2½ dozen balls

4 ounces blue cheese
1 pound ground beef
¼ cup dairy sour cream
¼ teaspoon dill

¼ teaspoon pepper
¼ teaspoon salt
2½ cups cooking oil

Crumble blue cheese in a bowl. Set aside. Combine ground beef, sour cream, dill and seasonings. Form into small burgerettes, about a tablespoon each, with blue cheese in center. Heat oil in "Fry All". Drop 8 at a time into fryer for 2 minutes. Remove and drain in basket hooked on base. Repeat.
Yield: 24 balls

ORANGE GINGER SAUCE

¼ cup mayonnaise
¼ cup dairy sour cream
½ teaspoon freshly grated
   orange rind
1 tablespoon orange juice
½ tablespoon finely chopped
   crystallized ginger

1 tablespoon finely chopped
   cashew nuts
½ clove garlic, crushed
½ teaspoon soy sauce

Combine all ingredients and mix well. Refrigerate 1 hour or longer to blend flavors.
Yield: About ¾ cup sauce

2½ cups grated Cheddar cheese
1 cup fine breadcrumbs
2 tablespoons softened butter
2 eggs, beaten
½ teaspoon salt

1/8 teaspoon cayenne pepper
1 teaspoon Worcestershire sauce
Paprika
2½ cups cooking oil

Combine cheese, breadcrumbs, butter, beaten eggs, salt, cayenne pepper and Worcestershire sauce. Mix well. Form into 1" balls. Chill. When ready to cook, heat oil in "Fry All". Roll balls in paprika, coating lightly. Drop a few at a time into hot deep fat and cook for 2 minutes. Remove and drain in basket hooked on base. Repeat.

Yield: About 2½ dozen balls

CHOCOLATE DOUGHNUT DROPS

2½ cups cooking oil
1 egg
2 tablespoons sugar
½ teaspoon salt
1 tablespoon melted butter
½ ounce baking chocolate, melted

¾ cup flour
1 teaspoon baking powder
¼ teaspoon cinnamon
3 tablespoons milk
Confectioners' sugar

Heat oil in "Fry All". Beat egg; add sugar, salt, butter and chocolate. Beat well. Sift flour, baking powder and cinnamon together; stir into chocolate mixture. Add milk and mix well. Drop by tablespoonsful into deep hot fat; fry until browned. Drain in basket hooked on base. Repeat. Sprinkle with confectioners' sugar.

Yield: About 1½ dozen

2½ cups cooking oil
1 small can water chestnuts,
    drained well
⅔ cup flour
¼ teaspoon garlic powder

¼ teaspoon salt
1 egg, beaten
1 tablespoon melted butter
⅓ cup beer

Heat oil in "Fry All". Pat water chestnuts dry. Sift flour, powdered garlic and salt together. Combine beaten egg, melted butter and beer; stir in sifted ingredients. Add a tablespoon of additional beer at a time to get desired consistency. Dip water chestnuts into batter and then drop into deep hot fat. Fry several at a time until golden. Remove and drain in basket hooked on base. Repeat until all are fried.

Yield: About 1 dozen

APPLESAUCE DOUGHNUTS

1 egg
⅓ cup sugar
⅓ cup applesauce
1 teaspoon grated lemon rind
2 teaspoons melted butter
1⅓ cups flour

½ teaspoon baking soda
½ teaspoon baking powder
¼ teaspoon nutmeg
¼ teaspoon salt
2½ cups cooking oil
Confectioners' sugar

Beat egg. Gradually add sugar, beating constantly. Add applesauce, lemon rind and butter. Sift together flour, baking soda, baking powder, nutmeg and salt; add to applesauce mixture. Mix well. Place dough in waxed paper; chill. Roll out ½ inch thick on a lightly floured board. Cut out doughnuts with floured cutter. Heat oil in "Fry All". Fry two at a time in deep hot fat for about 3 minutes or until golden brown, turning as they fry. Drain in basket hooked on base. Repeat. Sprinkle with confectioners' sugar.

Yield: About 1 dozen

2½ cups cooking oil

3 bananas

1 cup flour

2 teaspoons baking powder

1½ tablespoons sugar

¼ teaspoon salt

3 tablespoons milk

1 teaspoon lemon juice

1 egg, beaten

Confectioners' sugar

Heat oil in "Fry All". Mash bananas. Combine flour, baking powder, sugar and salt; add to bananas, alternating with milk. Stir in lemon juice. Add beaten egg. Drop by tablespoonsful into deep hot fat and fry until golden brown. Drain in basket hooked to base. Repeat until all batter is fried. Sprinkle with confectioners' sugar.

Yield: 4 to 6 servings

DEEP-FRIED APPLE FRITTERS

2½ cups cooking oil

1 cup sifted flour

1½ teaspoons baking powder

1¼ teaspoons salt

¼ teaspoon nutmeg

¼ teaspoon cinnamon

1 egg

⅓ cup milk

1 tablespoon melted butter

3 large apples, pared, cored, and
    sliced into ½" rings

Heat oil in "Fry All". Sift together flour, baking powder, salt, nutmeg and cinnamon. Beat egg; add milk and melted butter. Stir dry ingredients into egg mixture, beating until smooth. Dip apples in batter and fry a few at a time for 3-4 minutes, or until brown. Drain in basket hooked on base. Repeat.

Yield: 6 servings

2½ cups cooking oil
8 slices stale bread
¾ cup strong coffee
2 tablespoons brown sugar
¼ teaspoon salt
1 egg, beaten

¼ cup heavy cream
1 cup fine breadcrumbs
¼ teaspoon cinnamon
1 egg
¼ cup milk

Heat oil in "Fry All". Slice bread into 1" strips. Combine coffee, sugar, salt, 1 beaten egg and heavy cream; dip bread strips into this mixture, then into breadcrumbs mixed with cinnamon, then into egg beaten with milk, and finally into breadcrumbs again. Drop into deep hot fat and fry until golden. Repeat until all are fried. Drain in basket hooked on base.

Yield: 6 to 8 servings

Index

Recipes for "Little Mac" and "Double Mac" are set in regular type; recipes for "Fry All" are set in **bold** type.